SOME MINOR CHARACTERS IN THE NEW TESTAMENT

SOME MINOR CHARACTERS IN THE NEW TESTAMENT

BY

PROFESSOR A. T. ROBERTSON, Litt.D.,

CHAIR OF NEW TESTAMENT INTERPRETATION IN THE SOUTHERN
BAPTIST THEOLOGICAL SEMINARY, LOUISVILLE, KENTUCKY

BROADMAN PRESS
NASHVILLE, TENNESSEE

To

JOHN R. SAMPEY

My Beloved Friend
and Colleague for
Forty Years

These chapters have appeared mainly in *The Expositor* (Cleveland), *Church Management, The Moody Monthly, The Biblical Review,* and *The Record of Christian Work,* and are reproduced with the consent of these journals.

PREFACE

These sketches of various persons in the New Testament not treated formally in my other books have been an interesting by-play in my life-work. There are enough more for another volume. It has not yet been possible for me to write out the contemplated book on Simon Peter. A score of other volumes have cried out in me that may or may not see the light of day. The New Testament is the most gripping book in all the world for sheer human interest and charm.

A. T. ROBERTSON.

CONTENTS

CHAPTER I

NICODEMUS THE TIMID SCHOLAR

IT is the Fourth Gospel alone that tells us about Nicodemus and we catch only three glimpses of him (John 3:1–21; 7:45–52; 19:38–42). But his character is drawn with deftness and clearness. Each time he acts in perfect accord with the pictures drawn in the other places. The bold outline is not difficult to trace. He was a Pharisee and member of the Sanhedrin. These two items tell a great deal. The Sanhedrin had both Pharisees and Sadducees in the membership in nearly equal proportion. But the chief priest who presided over the meetings was Caiaphas, a Sadducee. There were many kinds of Pharisees. They are described in my Princeton lectures, *The Pharisees and Jesus*. Most of them were hostile to Jesus, but some were friendly and more open-minded.

Nicodemus is the first Pharisee who manifests a kindly spirit toward Jesus. Evidently he was a man far above the average in endowments of nature. He felt the appeal of Jesus at the very time that the men of his class were lined up against him. He was not willing to join in the outcry against Jesus because he had made a protest against the abuses of the temple worship. As a matter of fact the Sadducees were more responsible for the graft and coarse merchandise carried on right in the temple precincts (John 2:14), the enclosure (*to hieron*), not the sanctuary (*ho naos*). But the soul of Jesus rose in revolt at the desecration of his Father's house right before his eyes (2:16). The Jews challenged the authority of Jesus after they had fled before his wrath. But Jesus stood his ground and gave them as a proof of his Messianic authority the promise of his Resurrection which they did not understand. What did Nicodemus think of this claim of Jesus? We are not told, but we do know that many were carried away by the spectacle of a new rabbi from Nazareth who challenged and routed the whole ecclesiastical organization in Jerusalem. It was daring and it was magnificent, but it meant relentless hostility on the part of the Sanhedrin towards this revolutionary upstart who had charged them with connivance at desecration of the temple of God and who had actually said "My Father" in justification of his deed.

But Jesus was cautious and unwilling to credit this sudden enthusiasm which was without prop-r understanding of the real nature of the Kingdom of God which he was proclaiming and of his own relation to it. John's Gospel (2:23-5) contains an arresting statement of Christ's knowledge of human nature and of each man in particular. He means that Jesus understood men in a way not true of other men. Hence Jesus would not trust himself to these loud and impulsive believers (2:24).

They believed (aorist indicative, punctiliar action) on Jesus, but he refused to believe in them (imperfect indicative of the same verb, *pisteuo*).

It was in this critical atmosphere at the passover that Nicodemus, the Pharisee and member of the Sanhedrin, paid Jesus a secret visit by night, probably to his tent on the Mount of Olives. It required some courage at such a time when the men of his class had already taken an open stand against Jesus as an ignorant upstart and deceiver for a man like Nicodemus to show any interest in him. He did not wish to lose caste with his colleagues in the Sanhedrin. He did not court controversy. He was evidently a shy man as many scholars are. Nicodemus was a scholar in Jewish lore, probably a graduate of the theological school of Hillel in Jerusalem. It has often required courage in schools of learning for a scholar to take an open and active interest in Christ and in Christianity. There is fear of one's cult that is very real to-day. The situation in the schools of America is very much better than it was a hundred or more years ago among teachers and students. There are some teachers in our schools who take pleasure in ridiculing the deity of Christ and organized church life. But there have always been many scholars, more now than ever, who rejoice in glad and full worship of Jesus as Lord and Savior. School life brings a great many problems for the intellect and the soul. It is true that Nicodemus came to Jesus by night, but he came. He felt that Jesus had something that he did not possess and that he wanted. Nicodemus had watched the work of Jesus in Jerusalem and had deliberately made up his mind independently in spite of the prejudice against Jesus that he had the approval of God on his work.

It is possible that John, the author of the Fourth Gospel, was present and heard the conversation between Nicodemus and Jesus. Nicodemus explained why he had come: "Rabbi, I know (he says 'we,' probably literary plural, and he calls him 'rabbi' by courtesy, though Jesus was not a school man) that you have come from God as a teacher (a marvelous admission from the Jewish rabbi); for no one is able to go on doing (present infinitive *poiein*) these signs which you are doing, unless God be with him." It was not just one miracle, but a great many that Nicodemus had tested himself. The proof to Nicodemus was conclusive that Jesus wrought these signs by the power of God. Later the Pharisees will suggest that Jesus was in league with Beelzebub and wrought his miracles by the power of the devil. But even then they did not deny the reality of the cures. The signs merely enraged the enemies of Jesus who had already prejudiced the case against him. But Nicodemus was a Pharisee who did his own thinking and was anxious to be fair. He was not opposed to new truth just because it disturbed the equilibrium of his traditional theology. He wanted to get at the facts and so came to Jesus instead of merely listening to the misconceptions circulated about him and his work. If sceptics to-day would only go to Christ himself, with the right attitude of heart, they would find fresh light for many problems.

The answer of Jesus touches the real difficulty of Nicodemus of which he was not himself aware. As a Pharisee Nicodemus was looking for a political Kingdom under a political Messiah. But Jesus proclaimed a spiritual Kingdom, the reign of God in the heart that began with a new birth. "Verily, verily, I tell you, unless one be born again (or from above), he is not able to see (get to see, ingressive aorist infinitive) the Kingdom of God." But this idea was a shock to Nicodemus. He did not see that Jesus was speaking of a different sort of Kingdom and hence he thought only of physical birth when Jesus spoke of being born again or from above. There is no one so hard to teach as the man whose mind is already filled with error. So Nicodemus made a reply that seems stupid to us, but was intensely real to him: "How can a man be born when he is old? Is he able (surely not) to enter a second time into the womb of his mother and be born?" The gulf between Nicodemus and Jesus seems impassable. It is a tragedy to see a choice mind like that of Nicodemus befogged by error so patent.

But Jesus perseveres with patience and persistence. He tries a new form of his statement. Pure spiritual birth like the new birth was plainly outside of the range of the mind of Nicodemus. He was a Pharisee and used to symbolism in rites and ceremonies. Hence Jesus put the thing in a way that seems to have helped Nicodemus, though it has raised a fresh problem for modern men: "Verily, verily I tell you, unless one be born of water and of the Spirit, he is not able to enter the Kingdom of God. That which is born of the flesh is flesh, and that which is born of the Spirit is spirit. Do not wonder that I said to you, 'You must be born again.' The wind blows where it wills, and you hear the sound of it, but you do not know whence it comes and where it goes. So is every one who is born of the Spirit." We are puzzled by the placing of "water" here before "Spirit" as a necessity to entering the Kingdom of God. But Nicodemus was troubled about "Spirit." He was thinking only of the physical birth. On the whole it is probable that by "water" Jesus refers to baptism. John the Baptist preached repentance and practiced the baptism of those who confessed their sins. When Jesus repeats the point to Nicodemus he drops any mention of water: "You must be born again." This looks as if it was mentioned once in order to help Nicodemus understand that Jesus referred to spiritual birth as symbolized by baptism, not that baptism was essential to the new birth. Some, indeed, take "water" here to refer to the physical birth, since Jesus goes on to explain the two kinds of birth, physical and spiritual. In that case there would be no reference to baptism at all. Clearly it is the necessity of the new birth alone that Jesus is explaining to Nicodemus. Jesus tries to help Nicodemus again about the nature of the new birth of the Spirit by using the word for spirit (*pneuma*) in its original sense of wind with all its mystery of movement. Surely Nicodemus would now be able to grasp the idea of Jesus.

But Nicodemus could only make the rather dazed reply: "How can these things come to pass?" It was clearly beyond his intellectual horizon. So Jesus turns on Nicodemus with a rather sharp retort, but with the utmost kindness: "Are you the teacher of Israel and yet you do not know these things?" That question would cut to the quick, but Jesus meant that it should cut because the mind of Nicodemus with all his candor and sincerity seemed incapable of grasping spiritual truth. He was bound still in the clasp of Pharisaic formalism and ceremonialism. Jesus gave Nicodemus this electric jolt to shake him free if possible. So Jesus went on: "Verily, verily I tell you that I am speaking what I know (literary plural) and I am bearing witness to what I have seen, and yet you do not accept my witness." Here Jesus claims experimental knowledge concerning the spiritual realm. That is a scientific method and it should have appealed to a scholar like Nicodemus. But Jesus proceeded: "If I told you the earthly things and you do not believe, how will you believe if I tell you the heavenly things?" The new birth belongs to "the earthly things," taking place here on earth. "The heavenly things" include the Incarnation, the Atoning Death of Christ, God's redemptive love and grace (3:13–17). There was no reply from Nicodemus. It is not clear precisely where the words of Jesus cease and where the Evangelist goes on with his narrative. But evidently Nicodemus felt that he had gone into water beyond his depth. He was silenced, but apparently not yet convinced. Incredulity still held him fast. He could not reconcile the things that Jesus had said with his theological system. It would require time for Nicodemus to think through the problems raised by his interview with Jesus. One can imagine Nicodemus cautiously going away in the dark with many a shy glance to see if any one had observed his presence at the tent of the Rabbi from Nazareth.

It is probably a year and a half before we have a further note about Nicodemus in John's Gospel. It is at the feast of tabernacles just six months before the end of Christ's ministry when he appears in Jerusalem after a considerable absence. Jesus was there at a feast mentioned in John 5:1 and the feeling against him rose to fever heat and the Jewish leaders actually tried to kill him because he not only violated their rules about the Sabbath, but he actually made himself equal with God (John 5:18). Hence he remained away from Jerusalem. But now he did come and found the people divided in sentiment, though the friends of Jesus were awed through fear of the Sanhedrin (John 7:13). Finally the Sanhedrin sent officers to arrest Jesus and bring him before the body for trial (7:32). But, when they came, they did not bring Jesus. In amazement the Pharisees asked: "Why did you not bring him?" (7:45).

The officers, Roman soldiers as they were, calmly replied: "Never man spoke like this man" (7:46). Then it was that the Pharisees lost all control of themselves and said to the Roman officers: "Have you also gone astray? Did any one of the rulers believe on him or of the Pharisees? But this crowd that do not know the law are accursed." It would be hard to find elsewhere so much venom in so few words. They shouted their scorn at Roman officers being led off by an ignorant upstart from Galilee. Nobody but the *am-ha-aretz* (like our "clod-hoppers" or uncouth backwoodsmen) had followed Jesus. Not a single one of the leading Pharisees or rulers had believed on him. This last statement was an unconscious challenge to Nicodemus who had kept his secret well. He had slowly come closer to faith in Jesus as the Messiah, though he had taken no public stand for Christ. But manifestly Nicodemus winced under the words that not one of the rulers or of the Pharisees believed on Jesus. Nicodemus was both a Pharisee and a ruler and now he did secretly believe on him. Was he ready to take an open stand in the Sanhedrin for Jesus and own him as the Messiah of promise? Not that and not yet. He knew that, if he did, he would be ostracized and driven from the Sanhedrin. Later John will say: "Nevertheless, however, many of the rulers did believe (aorist tense) on him, but because of the Pharisees would not confess (imperfect tense) him that they might not become outcasts from the synagogue, for they loved the glory of men more than the glory of God"

(John 12:42–3). These are stinging words, it is true, but they correctly describe the attitude of men of the official class whose judgment was convinced that Jesus was the Messiah, though they lacked the courage to say so and pay the price of such courage. The lines were clearly and sharply drawn against Jesus in Jerusalem. What was Nicodemus to do? What did he do? He was unwilling to remain silent. He was afraid to avow his faith. He took a middle course. He would at least stand up for the legal rights of Jesus as he would for those of any man. So he ventured to raise a point of law. He put it clearly and sharply and all saw at once the bearing of the point: "Does our law condemn the man except it first hear from him and get knowledge of (ingressive aorist) what he is doing?" The very form of the question expects the negative answer. It was a sound legal principle and absolutely unanswerable. No one tried to answer it. Instead of that the other members of the Sanhedrin stormed at Nicodemus: "Are you also of Galilee? Search and see that no prophet comes out of Galilee." They passed by the matter of common justice mentioned by Nicodemus and made a personal thrust at him. They sneer at him as a mere ignorant Galilean like the mob and actually say that no prophet comes out of Galilee, an obvious untruth. But religious hatred knows no bounds. Nicodemus apparently lapsed into silence. He had cleared his conscience and had made himself a marked man. He would be under suspicion, though he kept his place in the Sanhedrin by keeping still as before.

Nicodemus is not heard from again till Jesus is dead upon the Cross. Two members of the Sanhedrin come forward late Friday afternoon to give decent burial to the body of Jesus. Joseph of Arimathea had been a secret disciple "because of fear of the Jews" (John 19:38). He was a rich man with a new tomb and he had not consented to the dreadful deed of the Sanhedrin (Luke 23:51). He asked Pilate for the body of Jesus that it might not be buried in the potters' field. Then it was that Nicodemus, another secret disciple in the Sanhedrin, stepped forward and took his stand by the side of Joseph of Arimathea. He brought a mixture of myrrh and aloes. These two men of scholarship and wealth now in the hour of deepest shame for Jesus openly avowed their love for him and confidence in him. How they felt now about his claims to be the Messiah we do not know. But they at least took up their cross when the apostles had fled. They gave Jesus dignified and honorable burial in Joseph's new tomb to the north of Jerusalem in the garden (John 19:41). The tomb was hewn out of a rock (Mark 15:46) and may have been the one now shown there near Gordon's Calvary. They rolled a great stone against the door of the tomb and went their way (Matt. 27:60). One may wonder if Nicodemus did not have many a pang in his heart that he had waited so long to take an open stand for Jesus at whatever cost.

At any rate it was some comfort to make small amends for his tardy confession by what he had now done. There are always those who will lay flowers on the coffin who gave none during life. And yet we must not be too harsh in our judgments of men. God sees the whole and we see only a part. Nicodemus was in a difficult place as many a man is to-day. He did at last show his colors for Christ.

CHAPTER II

ANDREW THE MAN OF DECISION

IT is the Fourth Gospel that tells most about Andrew, though we catch glimpses of him also in the Synoptic Gospels. He is not one of the outstanding figures among the twelve apostles, but he is very far from being a figurehead. He is a good specimen of the man of average gifts who had more than ordinary energy and who uses what gifts he has steadily and zealously. He comes from Bethsaida of Galilee and has a Greek name like Philip. The Greek language was spoken in Galilee as well as Aramaic and this fact may account in part for his name. He was not a Greek, for he was the brother of Simon Peter (Cephas). The name means "manly" from *aner*. We have the same proper name in English as that of Dr. Basil Manly, one of the first professors in the Southern Baptist Theological Seminary. It is clear that Andrew deserved his name and lived up to it. His father's name was John. He was engaged in the fishing business in Capernaum with his brother Simon and the brothers James and John. They were partners together and had hired men to help in the work. There must have been a regularly organized company including Zebedee the father

of James and John. In Capernaum Andrew lived
with his brother Simon who was married (Mark
1:29).

HE FELT THE PULL OF JOHN'S MISSION

Andrew was attracted to Bethany beyond Jordan by the preaching of John the Baptist as so
many others had been. It is even possible that
Andrew and Simon came with the crowd that included Philip of Bethsaida and Nathanael of Cana.
These towns were near to Nazareth and one may
wonder if Jesus, the carpenter of Nazareth, came
along with the same caravan. At any rate they are
all at Bethany beyond Jordan at the same time
when John the Baptist bears his remarkable and
stirring witness to the Messiahship of Jesus on
two successive days as the Lamb of God that takes
away the sin of the world and as the Son of God
(John 1:29–51). Andrew along with the rest felt
the pull of John's mission and message. He had
come close to the Baptist on one of the days at
Bethany, so close that he could hear distinctly the
Baptist's striking testimony to Jesus as the Messiah.

Andrew has the further distinction of being the
first one who followed Jesus as Messiah. That is
honor enough for any man. To be sure, the Baptist
had done so, but that is different. The Baptist was
the forerunner and had proclaimed the coming of
the Messiah before he saw Jesus on the banks of
the Jordan. He had recognized Jesus and had bap-

tized him and now he had publicly identified Him
as the Messiah after denying to the committee from
the Sanhedrin that he himself was the Messiah.
But there was as yet no rush of the people after
Jesus. The Baptist said: "In the midst of you
stands one whom you know not, one coming after
me, the latchet of whose sandal I am not worthy
to untie" (John 1:26). But where was He? One
day Andrew and another of John's disciples, who
was apparently John the brother of James, saw
John the Baptist point to Jesus of Nazareth with
a look of rapture and of longing that sent Andrew
and John after Jesus. It was a new experience for
Jesus and He turned sharply upon Andrew and
John and demanded what they wanted. The new
followers wanted further conversation, not controversy, and Jesus invited them to come and see
Him in His stopping-place at Bethany. It was a
memorable occasion, for they spent the day with
Jesus from ten o'clock in the morning (Roman
time), all that day (accusative case in the Greek,
extent of time). Andrew decided quickly to act
on the words of the Baptist and John joined him.
This quick decision is characteristic of Andrew.
If the Baptist meant what he said, the thing to
do was to leave the Baptist and go to Jesus.

HE STARTED THE PROCESSION OF THE CENTURIES

That is the way the testimony of the Baptist
struck the practical Andrew. He had come from
Galilee to see and hear the Baptist whose fame

had filled all the land. And now the Baptist had
sent him after one from Nazareth which is not
far from Bethsaida, his own town. To many this
would have been an insuperable difficulty as it
was a stumbling block to Nathanael (John 1:46).
Probably Andrew did not know at the moment
who Jesus was nor that He came from Nazareth.
He acted solely on the enthusiastic witness of the
Baptist whose disciple he had already become. But
that day with Jesus in his tent or in his khan
opened a new world to Andrew. He gave Jesus his
whole heart. The Baptist was right as Andrew now
knew by personal experience. Andrew had led the
way along the path that millions were to travel
in the coming ages, the "Jesus road" as the Indians
call it now. Andrew took the Baptist at his word
and started the procession of the centuries. In
every movement some one is the first to act, the
quickest to respond, to take the decisive step, to
cross the Rubicon.

But Andrew also is the first who won another
to Jesus as Messiah. He not simply is the first
who did it, but he did it as the first thing after
his own conviction that Jesus was the Messiah.
The correct text is *proton* which means the first
thing that he did, but some manuscripts read
protos, which would mean that he was the first
who did a thing like this, probably implying that
John did it also with his own brother James, but
after Andrew saw Simon. Both things are true
of Andrew. He was the first to win a convert and
he did it before he did anything else. It is note-

worthy also that his first convert was his brother
Simon. There are proverbial obstacles in the way
of spiritual approach to those who are kin to us
or who are closely connected by business ties. But
Andrew did not hesitate a moment. It was a startling piece of news that he had to tell to Simon and
he made it short: "We have found the Messiah."
The Baptist had raised expectations on every hand
about the Messiah, but he had not pointed Him
out to the people at large. Andrew and John had
been fortunate enough to catch the Baptist in the
act of identifying Jesus as the Messiah. Now their
own experience confirmed the witness of the Baptist. It was momentous, if true. But was it true?
Simon was a disciple of the Baptist, but he had
not seen Jesus and he was sceptical, no doubt,
though he knew that the Baptist had announced
that the Messiah was at hand.

IT WAS NOT EASY

It was probably not easy for Andrew to get
Simon to come to see Jesus. He was evidently unable to convince him without doing so. He was too
wise to risk it all on argument. Somehow he
brought Simon to Jesus. That was more than half
the battle. Andrew was acting again on his own
initiative. He was blazing a new trail. He was
learning how to lead his own brother into the love
and knowledge of Jesus Christ. He had no rules
to go by and no teacher to guide him. But he won
his man to Christ. If Andrew had done nothing

else in his life than this one act, he would deserve
the gratitude of Christians through all the ages.
He brought Simon to Jesus and opened the way
for the wonderful career of the man who, after
the death of Jesus, sprang to the front as the
leader of the apostles and who has left such a
deep mark upon the history of Christianity. The
greatest act of many a life is just this thing, to
win one great soul to Christ. It is practically always done by personal work and it is work that
any one can do. Andrew at this time was just a
layman, not a preacher.

So Andrew became a disciple of Jesus. Disciple
means learner under a teacher. He was not yet
one of the twelve apostles, but he was apparently
with Jesus at the wedding at Cana (John 2:2),
in Capernaum for a brief space (John 2:12), at
the first passover in Jerusalem (John 2:13, 17).
Like the other disciples he saw at Cana the mani-
festation of the glory of Jesus in His first miracle
that increased their faith. He saw the first clash
of Jesus with the Jerusalem ecclesiastics and recalled with the other disciples the saying of the
Psalmist (69:10) : "The zeal of thine house shall
eat me up." But, also like the rest, he did not comprehend what Jesus meant by raising "this temple
in three days" till after the resurrection of Jesus
(John 2:22). But these early days of the kingdom
of God on earth were wondrous to Andrew who
had had his share in starting the ball to rolling.
He may not have met Nicodemus, but he did wonder with the others that Jesus would talk in public

with a woman at Sychar in Samaria (John 4:27) and at the strange passion for souls that took away the hunger of the body (4:32).

THE CALL TO SERVICE

But Andrew had not yet given up his business as a fisherman. It was not until Jesus saw the two pairs of brothers washing their nets by the Sea of Galilee that He gave them a definite call to give up their business and to devote their time exclusively to His service, to the work of winning souls: "Come ye after me, and I will make you to become fishers of men" (Mark 1:17). That call has come to many laymen since Jesus invited Andrew and Simon, James and John, to stop making money and to make men. So "they left all and followed him" as learners and preachers, not yet as apostles in the technical sense. Soon Andrew, who lived with Simon and his family in Capernaum (Mark 1:29) saw ample proof of the power of Jesus in the very home where he lived. The mother-in-law of Simon was healed of a fever and that evening at sunset "all the city was gathered at the door" (Mark 1:33) of Andrew's house to see Jesus heal the procession of the sick as they passed by. Andrew probably shared in the perplexity of Peter early next morning when the crowds came again and found Jesus gone to a desert place to pray. It is plain that Andrew's part in the work was quiet. He saw Jesus defy the Pharisees from Jerusalem when He healed the paralytic let down through the roof of the house of Andrew and Peter (Mark 2:2).

It is small wonder that Andrew was included in the number of the twelve apostles carefully and prayerfully chosen by Jesus. He had already proven his worth to the cause of Christ. In the four lists of the twelve Andrew always appears in the first four. Mark's Gospel and Acts put him in the fourth place, while Matthew and Luke name him second just after Simon Peter. It was soon plain to all that Simon was more gifted than his older brother Andrew who yet had brought Simon to Jesus. There is nowhere a trace of jealousy on the part of Andrew toward Simon. He probably knew the weaknesses of Simon only too well as brothers always do, but he found joy in the prominence and leadership of Simon, and kept on doing his humble work.

A PRACTICAL TURN OF MIND

But it was not work that was useless or that any one could do. When the disciples propose to Jesus that he send the multitudes away on the slopes near Bethsaida Julias, Jesus proposes to Philip that something be done to feed them. Philip was at a loss as were the rest except Andrew who with his practical turn of mind made the suggestion to Jesus about the lad with five barley loaves and two fishes (John 6:8f.). The suggestion seemed like a forlorn hope even to Andrew, but the point is that Andrew made it. He would not give up without giving Jesus all the facts. Jesus at once took hold of the suggestion of Andrew and made it the starting point for working the wonderful miracle of feeding the five thousand. Andrew stands in clear light here. It is just the man like Andrew, more often a woman, who sees a little thing that can be done that turns the scale. To be sure, Andrew did not work the miracle. Jesus has all the glory for that, but Andrew found the boy who had the few loaves and fishes that the Master Workman used.

WISDOM FOR AN EMERGENCY

Once again Philip shows his estimate of Andrew as a man of wisdom for an emergency. It was the last week of the public ministry in Jerusalem, on Monday, the day after the triumphal entry. Jesus is in the Temple teaching when some Greeks, who have come up to worship at the feast of the Passover, possibly God-fearers if not proselytes, approach Philip with a desire to meet Jesus of whom all at the feast are now speaking: "Sir, we desire to see Jesus." Now Jesus is just at hand, but Philip does not introduce the Greeks to Jesus, as we should do to-day with strangers who desire to meet the preacher. Instead of that Philip consults Andrew (John 12:22) as the one most likely to help him with light on this problem of bringing Greeks to Jesus. One wonders if Philip had not seen Jesus at work in Phoenicia when the Syro-Phoenician woman won her case with Jesus and when in Decapolis among the Greeks Jesus wrought miracles. But this is in Jerusalem right in the midst of the Temple. The middle wall of partition rises before Philip and between him and the Greeks as it rose before Simon Peter later on the house-top in Joppa (Acts 10). The problem was too great for Philip and it was too great for Andrew. So both Andrew and Philip come and tell Jesus, but apparently do not bring the Greeks. Andrew's wisdom failed Philip on this occasion. It was not equal to the task of removing race and religious prejudice. Race hatred and national jealousy and religious rivalry to-day create acute problems that tax the wisdom of the world. No one has understood this matter so profoundly as Jesus whose heart was so greatly agitated by the dilemma of Andrew and Philip. Jesus knew that only His Cross could break down the wall of prejudice between Jew and Greek. What Andrew and Philip thought of the agitation of Jesus we do not know nor what the Greeks understood by the tragic words of Jesus: "And I, if I be lifted up from the earth, will draw all men unto myself." But we know to-day that nothing but the love of Christ can make men of many nations love each other and be just toward all.

THE LAST WE HEAR OF HIM

Andrew appears only once more by name in the Gospels. It is on the Mount of Olives after Jesus had, as they passed out of the Temple for the last time, foretold the destruction of the wonderful building of whose beauty they had spoken to Jesus. The disciples evidently talked about these strange words as they passed on out of the gate and through the valley of Jehoshaphat and up the slope of the Mount of Olives. When Jesus sat down on the summit of the mountain, "Peter and James and John and Andrew" asked Jesus privately the meaning of his language (Mark 13:3f.). Here Andrew is mentioned last in the list of four by Mark. Whether Mark obtained his information in chapter 13 (the "Little Apocalypse") from Peter is not known. But no special significance need to be attached to the position of Andrew's name. He had evidently joined in the discussion on the way up the mountain.

There are many legends in the apocryphal writings about Andrew, all of which will be passed by in our picture. He is represented as preaching in Bithynia, in Scythia, in Greece, among the Kurds. There is an apocryphal "Acts of St. Andrew."

The only item of real value is the statement in the *Muratorian Fragment* which says: "The Fourth Gospel was written by one of the disciples. When his fellow-disciples and bishops urgently pressed him, he said: 'Fast with me for three days, and let us tell one another any revelation which may be made to us, either for or against.' On the same night it was revealed to Andrew, one of the. apostles, that John should relate all in his own name, and that all should review." Whether this incident is true or not, it is in harmony with what we know of the character and work of Andrew.

The story is that he was crucified in Achaia by the proconsul Eges whose wife had been estranged from him by the preaching of Andrew. Part of the cross of Andrew is now shown in Rome for those who can believe it to be genuine. A piece of his arm is reported to be in Scotland so that he is the patron saint of Scotland.

But the numerous legends cannot destroy the clearness and force of the picture of this noble man who was the very first to take a stand for Jesus as the Christ.

CHAPTER III

HEROD THE GREAT PERVERT, AS PRESENTED IN THE GOSPEL OF MATTHEW

THE interest of New Testament students in Herod the Great grows primarily out of the fact that Jesus was born in Bethlehem before his death in B. C. 4. Luke expressly states that the angel Gabriel appeared to Zacharias "in the days of Herod, King of Judea" (Luke 1:5). He does not say in so many words that Herod was still reigning when Jesus was born, but he implies it (Luke 2:1–4).

But in Matthew 2:1–23 Herod cuts quite a figure in the narrative concerning the birth of Jesus. The picture here drawn of Herod the King of Judea fits in precisely with the extended account of this ruler in Josephus, *Antiquities,* Books xiv–xvii. We are not concerned in this article to tell the whole story of Herod the Great, "Herod the Great in Sin" as Amelie Rives calls him in *"Herod and Mariamne,"* save as that story throws light on his conduct about the birth of Jesus.

Herod has had champions ever since Nicolaus of Damascus, whose extensive eulogy contributed so much to the pages of Josephus. The Emperor Augustus thought well of him for the most part and once planned to enlarge his domain since he was a man of such big soul. But in the end he lost caste with Augustus.

See how Matthew presents Herod when he hears of the birth of the new King of the Jews from the wise men from the east: "And when Herod the king heard it, he was troubled, and all Jerusalem with him" (Matt. 2:3). Books xvi and xvii of the *Antiquities* of Josephus throw a tragic light on these simple words. The third period of Herod's career, his decline and death, is told here (B. C. 19–4). Herod's two sons by Mariamne (Alexander and Aristobulus) were the heirs to the throne as belonging to the Maccabean line. Mariamne was the granddaughter of Hyrcanus II. The return of these two sons from Rome, where they had been sent to mingle in court circles, was the occasion of jealousy on the part of Salome, Herod's sister, who had an intense dislike for the Maccabees. Antipater, Herod's son by Doris, joined in the schemings that led finally to the death of both Alexander and Aristobulus. Antipater was named successor, but grew impatient and acually plotted to get Herod out of the way that he might get the throne the sooner. As a result, he was thrown into prison and finally put to death. Herod, before the death of Antipater, had made Antipas, his son by Malthace, his heir. It was apparently at this juncture, before the death of Antipater, that the visit of the Wise Men so disturbed the old and irritable tyrant. The idea of a new king, not one of his sons, upset Herod the Great very thoroughly. All Jerusalem was likewise disturbed.

The city was apprehensive about fresh manifestations of cruelty on the part of Herod the Great. The Roman Emperor and judges had winked at the death of the two sons by Mariamne (Alexander and Aristobulus). Augustus had made his famous pun on the death of these young men: "I would rather be Herod's hog than his son" (his *hus* than his *huios*). But that was not the beginning of Herod's cruelty. He had obtained Antony's consent to the death of the Maccabean Antigonus whom the Parthians had set up as king and high priest. He had put to death forty-five of the leaders in the Sanhedrin, sparing Pollio and Sameas. He had secured the drowning of the young high priest Aristobulus, the brother of Mariamne, grand-daughter of Hyrcanus II whom he married to consolidate his hold on the throne and the Jewish people. He had finally caught the aged Hyrcanus in a plot with the Arabians and secured his death. By the help of his sister, Salome, he had his beloved wife Mariamne put to death on trumped-up charges. He almost lost his mind for grief after the death of Mariamne. Then Alexandra, the mother of Mariamne, was put to death. The sons of Baba were likewise slain at the demand of Salome, to get the Maccabean adherents out of the way. Salome gratified her spite against her own husband, Costobar, by his divorce and then death. These family disturbances kept the court circles in Jerusalem in a turmoil and the people generally on the *qui vive*. Nobody knew what

Herod was likely to do when in one of his tantrums over family affairs. Josephus several times facetiously says that about this time Herod's family affairs grew worse and worse. There was suspicion on every side and nobody trusted anybody. Small wonder, therefore, that all Jerusalem was troubled over the new disturbance in the mood of Herod the Great, one of the most whimsical and cruel and selfish tyrants of all time.

Herod first "gathered together all the chief priests and scribes of the people" and "inquired of them where the Christ should be born" (Matt. 2:4). He probably knew something of the Messianic expectation of the Jewish people, but had apparently taken no personal interest in the matter. He was an Idumean by birth and a nominal Jew since the Idumeans had been conquered by John Hyrcanus I. But he was actually without religious interest or concern. His present agitation was not due to personal interest in the birth of the Jewish Messiah, but purely to the peril to his own wishes about his successor. The appeal to the Jewish ecclesiastical leaders was to secure information for his own conduct, not with a view to helping the wise men in their worship of the Messiah.

The sly shrewdness of Herod about the request of the wise men is in precise accord with his conduct concerning the reports about the various victims of his jealous rage. "Then Herod privily called the wise men, and learned of them carefully what time the star appeared" (Matt. 2:7). He appeared on the surface to approve of the aim of the wise men and to desire to coöperate with them, though he had already given way to his violent emotions among the members of the household and court circles. "And he sent them to Bethlehem and said, Go and search out carefully concerning the young child; and when ye have found him, bring me word, that I also may come and worship him" (Matt. 2:8). There is an obvious untruth in the words of Herod. He had not the remotest idea of worshiping the Babe in Bethlehem if the wise men succeeded in finding the Messiah there according to Micah's prophecy. But he wished the wise men to think so and to make a report to him of the result of their search in order that he might then know how to proceed. Josephus gives ample proof of like duplicity on the part of Herod concerning the death of young Aristobulus and how Alexandra, the mother, was not deceived by reports of the "accidental" drowning of her son nor by the hypocritical tears of Herod and the grand funeral. So also Mariamne was not deceived by the double-dealing of Herod in his orders to have her put to death if he was not spared by Antony and then by Octavius. Matthew leaves us to infer that the wise men from the east, strangers to Palestine and to Herod, might have fallen into Herod's trap if they had not been "warned of God in a dream that they should not return to Herod" (Matt. 2:12). They may, to be sure, have heard something about the jealousy and cruelty of Herod's character since all Jerusalem was troubled. The dream would simply confirm the vague fears already entertained. At any rate "they departed into their own country another way," and Herod was left to draw his own conclusions about the young Messiah whether he was really in Bethlehem or not.

Joseph also probably was only too familiar with the reputation of Herod the Great. It is likely that the wise men told Joseph of the inquiry and command of Herod and of the dream which led them to leave Jerusalem and Herod to one side on their return home. At any rate the dream that came to Joseph was definite with a clear picture of the purpose of Herod: "Arise and take the young child and his mother, and flee into Egypt, and be thou there until I tell thee: for Herod will seek the young child to destroy him" (Matt. 2:13). There was no disobeying a clear command like that, even in a dream sent by God. It fell in precisely with all that was known of the imperious will of Herod who was unwilling to brook a rival even after his death. It began to look to Herod as if all his plans might go awry and no one of his sons might succeed him. Joseph lost no time in getting out of Herod's way with Mary and Jesus. He remained in Egypt with his precious charge till the death of Herod (Matt. 2:14). Under the circumstances that was only common prudence, but Joseph had direct revelation from God to strengthen his purpose.

But Matthew notes that the execution of the warning was none too soon, for Herod was not long in seeing that he had been outwitted by the wise men. A trickster is always angry when his trickery fails to work. "Then Herod, when he saw that he was mocked of the wise men, was exceeding wroth" (Matt. 2:16). The palace, no doubt, was a dangerous place even for the inmates who had learned how to avoid Herod in a time like this. He knew by intuition that the wise men had somehow seen through his suave phrases and had purposely avoided making a report to him concerning their search for the young Messiah. It might be possible, to be sure, that they had not succeeded in finding him. But then again they may have been unwilling to tell him because they had learned something of his conduct towards members of his own family. Herod was not willing to take any chances about so important a matter which might mean the thwarting of his own will. He did not know that a pretender to the throne had been born in Bethlehem, let alone the name of such a child there. It still seems incredible to some modern men that on mere suspicion Herod should have done so cruel a thing, for he "sent forth, and slew all the male children that were in Bethlehem, and in all the borders thereof, from two years old and under, according to the time which he had carefully learned of the wise men" (Matt. 2:16). He felt sure that the babe was not over two years old, though exactly how old he did not know. Hence he gave a blanket order for the slaughter of all the little boys as old as two years. We have no means of knowing the precise number that were slain, probably about twenty. The size of the community would certainly call for that number of infant boys. This slaughter of the innocent little boys would be incredible in the lives of most tyrants and criminals, but it causes no jar to one familiar with the life of Herod the Great as told by Josephus. It is objected by some writers that the account in Matthew's Gospel lacks confirmation by Josephus. The reply to that criticism is that this incident was a small item in the long life of Herod and had no particular interest to Josephus. What Josephus does tell about Herod makes the narration by Matthew highly credible. The talk about this latest exhibition of cruelty on the part of Herod would soon die down. The children that were put to death were probably for the most part in the homes of more or less obscure people who were not considered to have any particular rights by the king. It is revolting to us to think of the willful murder by a king of these helpless and harmless babies who lost their lives for the sake of and, in a sense, in the place of the Babe Jesus who had been taken away to Egypt. They were put to death because of the insane jealousy and anger of Herod about the birth of the Messiah in Bethlehem as Herod feared, according to the prophecy of Micah and the inquiry of the wise men. Probably Herod soon forgot the slaying of these little boys as too small a matter to occupy the thoughts of a king.

He was in serious trouble himself. He had a loathsome disease and sought in vain the benefit of the healing waters of Callirhoe. It is a pitiful picture that Josephus draws of the closing days of

the famous king of the Jews. He actually tried
to kill himself in order to get out of his misery.
He was determined that he should be mourned at
his funeral and seemed to know that nobody really
loved him, not even Salome, his sister who had
made him gratify her own hatreds and prejudices.
He gave command that a number of prominent
men should be slain in the event of his death in
order that there would certainly be general mourning in Jerusalem. His directions concerning a
splendid display at his funeral were carried out
very strictly. But there was no real grief at his
departure. He was despised alike by his own family
and by the Jewish people who felt that his successor could not be any worse than he had been.

The death of Herod the Great was B. C. 4 and
gives the proof that the birth of Jesus was before
that date. Joseph at once faced the problem of
returning to Palestine. He had feared to risk a
return while Herod was alive because his agents
might find it out and seek to kill the child Jesus.
"But when Herod was dead, behold, an angel of
the Lord appears in a dream to Joseph in Egypt,
saying, Arise and take the young child and his
mother, and go into the land of Israel; for they
are dead that sought the young child's life" (Matt.
2:20). Only Herod had died, so far as we know,
though it is possible that some of the assassins
sent by Herod to Bethlehem may have died also.
It is more likely, however, that the plural "they"
means only Herod who is referred to in this general way. The way now was open for the return.

So "he arose and took the young child and his mother, and came into the land of Israel" (Matt. 2:21). The first interest of the state authorities in the birth and life of Jesus was active hostility. Another Herod, Agrippa I, will later put James, the brother of John, to death and imprison Simon Peter (Acts 12:1). It has not been easy for the state to understand how to treat Christianity fairly. Real religious liberty has come at last in the United States and is needed by all the world.

Once back in Palestine Joseph found that Herod had changed his will again before he died. When Joseph fled from Bethlehem, the successor was to be Herod Antipas. "But when he heard that Archelaus was reigning over Judea in the room of his father, he was afraid to go thither; and being warned of God in a dream, he withdrew into the parts of Galilee, and came and dwelt in a city called Nazareth" (Matt. 2:22-3). We find in Josephus that at the last Herod had changed his will once more in a fit of uneasiness. No one of his sons was to get the whole kingdom as had been expected. All the schemings were in vain after all. Alexander and Aristobulus and Antipater were dead. Under the new will Archelaus, his son by Malthace, was to get Idumea, Judea and Samaria with the title of Ethnarch, while Herod Antipas, another son by Malthace, was to be Tetrarch of Galilee and Perea, and Herod Philip, his son by Cleopatra, of Jerusalem, was to be Tetrarch of Iturea and Trachonitis. It is plain that Joseph preferred Herod Antipas to Archelaus. The out-

come showed the wisdom of Joseph, for Archelaus
turned out to be the worst of Herod's sons, now
that Antipater was dead. Joseph "was afraid to
go thither" to Bethlehem under the rule of Archelaus. He was evidently apprehensive lest Archelaus
carry out the plan of Herod the Great and slay
the child Jesus on his return to Bethlehem. This
fear was confirmed by the warning in a dream.
One may wonder why Joseph planned to go back
to Bethlehem instead of to Nazareth where he had
his home and his business. It may be that Joseph
felt it was proper for the Messiah to be reared in
Bethlehem where he was born and where David
had lived as a youth. In Bethlehem also no question would be raised by gossip about the birth of
Jesus and the recent marriage to Mary. In the
nature of the case Joseph and Mary could not
tell the neighbors in Nazareth what the angel
Gabriel had told them. But the change of rulers
made Joseph and Mary decide to take no risk about
the life of the child. It was far better to endure
the wagging tongues of neighbors than to place
the life of the child Jesus in jeopardy in Bethlehem.

It is surprising to see what a part the wickedness
of Herod and his family played in the early events
in the life of Jesus as recorded in the Gospel of
Matthew. Because of Herod's jealous fears the
little male children of Bethlehem were slain, the
child Jesus was taken to Egypt and kept there
till the death of the tyrant. Because of the character of Archelaus Jesus lived in Nazareth instead
of Bethlehem and was called a Nazarene.

Archelaus is called king by Matthew, 2:22, in popular parlance, though he did not actually obtain the title. His title as Ethnarch was challenged by Salome and Herod Antipas. Salome failed in her effort to upset Herod's will and Archelaus became Ethnarch with the promise of the higher title in case of good behavior. But he did not make good and in ten years was recalled and Roman procurators ruled the province of Judea. There is little doubt that Jesus refers to the expedition of Archelaus to obtain the kingdom in the parable of the pounds in Luke 19.

It is plain that the picture of Herod the Great given in the Gospel of Matthew is of a piece with that drawn at length by Josephus. He was a selfish and a cruel man who really cared little for others save as they contributed to his own pleasure. He tried in a frantic manner to win the favor of the Jews by gifts in time of famine and by erecting fine buildings, especially the new temple in Jerusalem. The people distrusted his plans about this and would only agree to the tearing down of any portion when Herod was ready to replace it. The work, begun in B. C. 20, was not really completed till A. D. 65, but it bore Herod's name and was a very wonderful structure.

Herod was a Hellenist in his sympathies and tastes and introduced Greek games and built theaters and places for gymnastic exercises. As a result, he was disliked and distrusted by the Pharisees. He angered the Jews also by rebuilding Samaria which he called Sebaste. He made Cæsarea so attractive that the Romans made it the political capital of Palestine. Herod was a political opportunist of the first rank. He curried favor with the Romans and won the favor of Augustus to an astonishing degree. His Hellenizing practices were very irritating to the Pharisees, but he stood well with some of the Sadducees.

Herod undoubtedly had great talents of a certain sort. But ambition and lust reigned in his life. He had ten wives and was an absolute autocrat in his home and in his kingdom.

Distance lends enchantment to the view. After his death and the Roman procurator has taken the place of Archelaus, we find a party of Herodians whose policy was to restore the rule of the Herods. They hated the Pharisees very much, but came to hate Jesus more and were willing to conspire with the Pharisees to put Jesus to death (Mark, 3:6). Jesus warned the disciples against "the leaven of the Pharisees and the leaven of Herod" (Mark 8:15). On the last Tuesday in the Temple the Herodians combine with the Pharisees in trying to catch Jesus with the issue of giving tribute to Cæsar (Mark 12:13; Matt. 22:16).

Herod was a past master in intolerance and he was living up to his past when he acted as he did toward the magi and the babes in Bethlehem. The Roman Emperor Augustus was responsible by his new periodical census for the birth of Jesus in Bethlehem, though Augustus little knew that the chief interest in his census on the part of future centuries would be precisely this item connected with it. It can be said about Herod the Great that he did not know that he was stepping athwart the plans of Almighty God in his angry whim to kill the babes to prevent the expected Jewish Messiah from breaking his own will. Both Emperor and King seem like puppets on the stage in the larger purposes of God and yet each was true to his own nature and environment. No doubt the devil tried to use Herod to get rid of the child Jesus as he did use Judas and the Jewish ecclesiastics to compass his death at a later period. Herod was willing enough to play the devil's part as he had often done before. But God would not let Jesus die before his "hour" had come. That problem confronts each of us in the midst of malevolence and accidents on every hand. We can see the restraining hand of God in the sparing of the child Jesus, though Herod's guilt was just the same. But that is not to say that we can always see the hand of God in the path of the tornado, the earthquake, or the shipwreck. The picture of Herod is black enough in Josephus. It is made a bit blacker by the second chapter of Matthew's Gospel.

CHAPTER IV

CAIAPHAS THE BLINDED ECCLESIASTIC

CAIAPHAS challenges the interest of modern men because he was the high priest during the ministry of Jesus. He presided at the meeting of the Sanhedrin which tried Jesus and he took the lead in the opposition to Jesus towards the end. One wishes that there was more information available about his life. He was high priest from A. D. 18 when he was appointed by Valerius Gratus till A. D. 36 when he was removed by Vitellius. But he held his place for eighteen years which fact shows that he knew how to get along with the Roman officials. He was the son-in-law of Annas (Ananus) who was high priest from A. D. 7 to 14. Annas continued to be called high priest even after he was no longer in possession of the office (Luke 3:2, John 18:19–22; Acts 4:6). As a matter of fact Annas was the dominant force in the priestly party. In Luke 3:2 we find that "in the high-priesthood of Annas and Caiaphas" John began his ministry. In Acts 4:6 Annas is named before any one else: "And Annas the high priest was there, and Caiaphas, and John, and Alexander, and as many as were of the kindred of the high priest." Five of the sons of Annas, besides his son-in-law, Caiaphas, succeeded him as high priest. It is small wonder, therefore, that he continued to dominate the Sadducees even though no longer in office. While Caiaphas was the titular head, Annas was the moving spirit among the Sadducees.

But Caiaphas cannot be excused from his responsibilities in connection with Jesus. Caiaphas recognized the high standing of Annas by sending Jesus to him first (John 18:12–23), while he was gathering the Sanhedrin together for the full meeting and John's Gospel calls Annas here high priest. But Caiaphas in no sense tried to dodge his own leadership as the nominal high priest. We see Caiaphas in bold outline on three occasions in the New Testament.

When Jesus raised Lazarus from the grave at Bethany just east of Jerusalem, some of the Jews who had come over to comfort Martha and Mary (John 11:19), went and told the Pharisees what had happened (John 11:46). There was no effort to discredit the stupendous miracle. Jesus had said just a little while before: "If they hear not Moses and the prophets, neither will they be persuaded, if one rise from the dead." So now the Pharisees are not convinced of the Messianic power and claims of Jesus by the raising of Lazarus. Rather they see peril to their own position as the people flock to the side of Jesus. The situation calls for instant action on the part of the Sanhedrin to stop Jesus from raising dead people right at the door of Jerusalem. "The chief priests therefore and the Pharisees gathered a council" (John 11:47). It was a special meeting of the Sanhedrin at the call of both Sadducees (chief priests) and Pharisees, enemies and rivals in the Sanhedrin who are now united in face of the dangerous prestige of Jesus because of the raising of Lazarus in the presence of so many witnesses, many of whom had already believed on Jesus (John 11:45). The general sentiment was voiced: "What are we doing, for this man is doing many signs? It we let him thus alone, all men will believe on him and the Romans will come and will take away both our place and our nation" (John 11:47f). It was very adroit and fully justified the suddenly called meeting of the Sanhedrin. It was plain to all that the only way to save the nation was for the rulers to keep their positions. They piously put place before patriotism with frank naïveté. The Sadducees and Pharisees in the Sanhedrin have an instinctive feeling that the success of Jesus placed in jeopardy their own offices and the very existence of the nation. They looked upon Jesus as a dangerous revolutionist whose ambitions would probably embroil the nation with the Romans who would be only too glad of a pretext to destroy the city of Jerusalem. As a matter of fact the Romans did come and they took away the nation and robbed the rabbis of their place in the Sanhedrin which perished with the destruction of the temple, though it was revived later in Galilee with some modifications. The rabbis were right in the feeling that their very existence as a court was at stake. It is at this point that Caiaphas, the high priest, is first heard with a piece of oracular wisdom characteristic of the professional ecclesiastic who cares more for his own selfish interest than for anything else: "You do not know anything at all (probably true) nor do you consider that it is expedient for you that one man die in behalf of the people and not all the nation perish" (John 11:49f). Caiaphas spoke as the incarnation of selfishness, and put to the test by his subtle proposal the self-interest of all the other members of the Sanhedrin. He made the definite and concrete suggestion that the thing to do was to get Jesus out of the way in order to save the nation from the Romans. His plan was adopted by the Sanhedrin and after some weeks carried out, but it did not save the nation from the Romans. In fact, Jesus will one day predict the ruin of the nation for the very reason that they have decided to kill him. Worldly wisdom is not always wise, but often otherwise. Caiaphas proposed the easy way out, as many a deacon has done in a church trouble by pushing the pastor out in order to save the church. That may be best sometimes, but by no means always. It certainly did not so turn out about Jesus. Incidentally, Caiaphas uses the Greek preposition *huper* in the substitutionary sense, because he adds, "and not all the people perish." He actually offers Jesus as an involuntary sacrifice in order to save the Jewish nation. No question of right or wrong is raised. Whether Jesus deserves such a death or not is quite beside the issue. He can be made to contribute to the welfare of the Sanhedrin and of the nation by killing him. The philosophy of Caiaphas is that of many another pious scoundrel. He is perfectly willing to obtain peace by the ruin of another man. Caiaphas appears in an utterly despicable rôle that is in no sense relieved by the interpretation of the Evangelist that, as high priest, the language of Caiaphas had a prophetic meaning concerning the atoning death of Christ (John 11:51-2). That is all true enough, but Caiaphas did not mean it and he must be measured by his own motive which was wholly selfish and mean. His argument made an impression and stuck to his name (John 18:14). He carried his point and the Sanhedrin decided by formal vote to kill Jesus (11:53). They had planned it for a long time. Now it was only a matter of weeks. They made public proclamation for any one who saw Jesus come to the passover to reveal his whereabouts that they might arrest him (John 11:57). Perhaps this notice was posted as a placard in the temple courts. When the crowd gathered at Bethany to see Jesus and Lazarus, the rulers decided to kill both of them (12:10f).

Caiaphas comes to his glory at the trial of Jesus. The demonstration in favor of Jesus during the Triumphal Entry made the Sanhedrin pause in the attempt to kill Jesus during the passover feast because of the sympathy of the Galilean populace. So they held a meeting in the court of Caiaphas and decided to put off the death of Jesus till after the feast to avoid a tumult of the people (Matt. 26:3-5). In simple truth Caiaphas was frightened by the unexpected popularity of Jesus as the crowds in the temple hung on the words of Jesus

(Luke 21 :37f). It was Judas who came to the help of Caiaphas at this juncture and pointed out how Jesus could be arrested in the Garden of Gethsemane at night while at prayer and be tried and condemned before the people stirred in the morning. It was a clever scheme to make Jesus lose popular sympathy as a Messianic hero by a *fait accompli* with Christ as a condemned criminal. This could all be done "in the absence of the multitude." The treachery of Judas no doubt appeared to Caiaphas as a dispensation of Providence in favor of the Sanhedrin (Luke 22 :3–6). No wonder he was glad, and sealed the bargain with Judas by paying him the price of a slave.

It is plain that the task of getting Jesus condemned by the Sanhedrin fell to Caiaphas. Judas had Jesus arrested and turned him over bound to Annas first (John 18 :13), while Caiaphas gathered the Sanhedrin together in his house (Matt. 26 :57; Luke 22 :54). Then Annas sent Jesus on to Caiaphas (John 18 :24). Caiaphas presided and conducted the trial which was a prosecution rather than a trial. There was no indictment and no warrant and no opportunity for Jesus to have a lawyer or witnesses. The purpose of the Sanhedrin was to convict Jesus, not to find out the truth about him. Moreover, they sought for false witnesses in order to put Jesus to death (Mark 15 :55; Matt. 26 :60). The farcical trial took place at night instead of by day. Besides, the Sanhedrin no longer had the power of life and death as Caiaphas knew perfectly well and admitted to

Pilate (John 18:30). It is not made clear why the Sanhedrin condemned Jesus to death anyhow since it was futile without the approval of Pilate. But Caiaphas did not tell Pilate that the Sanhedrin had already condemned Jesus to death (Luke 23: 2; John 18:30). Pilate actually offered to turn Jesus over to them for trial (John 18:31), but they protest that they cannot put him to death and do not say that they have already condemned him to death. They do at least say that he ought by their law to die because he made himself the Son of God (John 19:7). Why then did the Sanhedrin go through the farce of a trial? Perhaps as protest against the Roman usurpation. Perhaps also as a means of gratifying personal resentment against Jesus who had defied them so utterly before the people.

But even so, the so-called trial by Caiaphas was a failure. The only testimony against Jesus with a semblance of truth was given by two witnesses who contradicted each other. It was a desperate situation and it would have ended the matter with the freedom of Jesus by a judge who cared for the facts and for truth and justice. But Caiaphas had staked all on a verdict now that by the treachery of Judas he had Jesus in his power. So with bluster and bravado this prejudiced ecclesiastic put Jesus on solemn oath before the Sanhedrin concerning his claim to be "the Christ, the Son of God" (Mark 14:61; Matt. 26:63). Caiaphas had no legal right to treat a prisoner thus. The whole trial violated Jewish legal procedure at every step.

But Caiaphas would stop at nothing. Jesus did not have to reply and convict himself by his own testimony. But he did reply on oath that he was the Messiah, the Son of God (Mark 14:62; Matt. 26:64). If he had kept silent now, as he had done before, that would have been interpreted as denial that he made such a claim. Hence Jesus took his life in his hands in his answer. It was not blasphemy for the Son of God to claim to be the Messiah. But the Sanhedrin would not agree that Jesus of Nazareth was the Messiah, the Son of God. Hence they called it blasphemy and condemned him to death which was now illegal for them and which judgment they could not execute. The Sanhedrin showed their glee at the result by conduct worthy of hoodlums or of "rough-necks" as they mocked and buffeted Jesus (Mark 14:65; Matt. 26:67f; Luke 22:63-5).

Caiaphas had carried his point against Jesus before the Sanhedrin and now had the far more difficult task of getting a conviction from Pilate. The Roman governors at least had to keep up the semblance of justice. Pilate bore an evil reputation and the Jews had many counts against him. All this made him afraid of the power of Caiaphas who could report him to Cæsar. But even so, Caiaphas did not have an easy time with Pilate who several times announced the innocence of Jesus and ought to have set him free. He would have done so but for the persistence of Caiaphas and of the Sanhedrin. They had adroitly accused Jesus of claiming to be "Christ a King" (Luke

23:2), and Pilate had to examine that charge though he soon saw that Jesus was no rival of Cæsar as a political ruler. At the end Pilate was disposed to set Jesus free, but the Jews cried out that they would tell Cæsar on him if he did (John 18:12). Then Pilate surrendered and Caiaphas and the Sadducees actually boasted of their loyalty to Cæsar: "We have no king but Cæsar" (John 18: 15). Caiaphas played a desperate game and carried it on to the end and took the blood of Jesus on his own head and the heads of the people and of their children (Matt. 27:25).

Caiaphas appears in the book of Acts also. The Sadducees took ill the bold preaching of Peter and John that Jesus had actually risen from the dead (Acts 4:2). The Sadducees took the lead in the death of Jesus though the Pharisees were the first to attack him and his teachings. The Sadducees are the first to arrest the apostles while for a time the Pharisees held off. The emphasis on the doctrine of the resurrection at first stressed the cleavage between the Sadducees and the Pharisees at this point. It might appear from Acts 4:6 that Annas was even more active in the persecution and arrest of Peter and John than Caiaphas. But certainly Caiaphas did his share in the formal meetings of the Sanhedrin. Peter boldly accused the Sanhedrin of the death of Jesus, "whom ye crucified" (Acts 4:10). Caiaphas and the rest resent the courage of Peter, but are helpless in the presence of the healed man and are full of scorn of the name Jesus (4:17f). The prohibition against preaching the resurrection of Jesus was useless and the Sadducees tried another arrest (Acts 5:17f), but Peter and the other apostles bluntly defied them: "We must obey God rather than men" (5:29). This time Gamaliel came to the rescue of the apostles and revealed a breach between Caiaphas and Gamaliel, or between the Sadducees and the Pharisees, on the doctrine of the resurrection.

It is probable that Stephen appeared for trial before Caiaphas also (Acts 9:1), though the glory or shame of Stephen's death rests with the Pharisees rather than with the Sadducees. Stephen stirred up the Pharisees as Peter had the Sadducees. The two parties came together again as in the trial and death of Jesus. So then the united Sanhedrin made short work of Stephen and did not wait this time for the approval of Pilate who may have already been recalled with no successor yet on hand. At any rate it was a case of mob law, or lynch law, that did not wait for a judicial process. Gamaliel made no protest in behalf of Stephen and Caiaphas let the Pharisees have their way as they would not in the case of Simon Peter.

It is probable also that Caiaphas gave Saul the papers to go to Damascus to arrest and bring before the Sanhedrin the Christians in that city (Acts 9:1). If so, Caiaphas presided in the numerous condemnations of men and women to death for the crime of being Christians under the leadership of young Saul. As this was a Pharisaic persecution, the leadership passed from Caiaphas to Saul, but there is no evidence that Caiaphas failed to coöperate with the zealous Pharisee who was trying to put an end to Christianity, an end much desired by Caiaphas.

Caiaphas remains a typical ecclesiastic who is blinded by prejudice and privilege. The light of the world shone around him and before him, but he could not see. If he had been blind in his physical eyes, it would not have been so bad (John 9: 41). He had spiritual blindness though he professed to be the spiritual leader of his people. There are none so blind as those who will not see. If the light within Caiaphas was darkness, how great was that darkness (Matt. 6:23). Caiaphas was an obscurantist who tried to stop the sun from shining. The religious reactionary always steps out boldly in front of the march of God through the ages. But in the end he is run over by the inevitable shining of the light which cannot be held back and which shines on forever. The furthest star shines on though millions of light-years away. But Caiaphas stood right in front of the Sun of Righteousness and denied that he saw anything. As a matter of fact he did not see what was before him. The eyes of his heart were not opened so that he could see. Having eyes he saw not and ears he heard not.

CHAPTER V

PILATE THE UNJUST JUDGE

THERE is no doubt at all about the weakness and the cowardice of Pilate. The story of the trial of Jesus shows the feebleness of the character of Pilate as recorded in each of the Gospels. Munkacsy's great painting, Christ before Pilate, seizes upon this feature with consummate power. Pilate there really appears to be on trial before Christ, as he is, in fact, condemned by the moral judgment of the world for his treatment of Jesus.

But late legends condone the conduct of Pilate and even credit him with becoming a Christian and he is enrolled among the saints in the Coptic Church. In particular, his wife, who is given the name of Claudia Procula or Procla, is identified with the Claudia of 2 Timothy 4:21 and October 27 is her calendar date in the Coptic Church. The message of Pilate's wife that he should have "nothing to do with that righteous man" (Matt. 27:19), probably explains the favorable opinion held by some Christians concerning Pilate's wife. It is best to pass by all the apocryphal accounts of Pilate such as the references in the Gospel of Peter (second century), the Gospel of Nicodemus (fourth century) containing the Acts of Pilate, and also pass by the Acts of Peter and Paul with the alleged (but spurious) letter or report of Pilate to Tiberius. The extant Acts of Pilate are spurious, though credited by some people to-day.

It is enough to draw our picture of Pilate from the Gospels and from Josephus and from Philo. It is plain from these writings that Pilate incurred the dislike of the Jews on many grounds (Philo, *Ad Gaium,* 38). Here Agrippa tells how Pilate hung gilt shields in the palace of Herod in Jerusalem on which were inscribed the names of the donor and of him in whose honor the shield was set up. The Jews were enraged at this and wrote to Tiberius who ordered Pilate to remove them. Philo quotes Agrippa as saying that the threat of the Jews "exasperated Pilate in the greatest possible degree, as he feared lest they might impeach him with respect to other particulars of his government—his corruption, his acts of insolence, his rapine, and his habit of insulting people, his cruelty, and his continual murder of people untried and uncondemned, and his never-ending, gratuitous, and most grievous inhumanity." This description can be discounted as partly Jewish hatred. But Josephus (*Ant.* XVIII. iii. 1; *War* II. ix. 2, 3) related how Pilate angered the Jews greatly by directing the Roman soldiers to go to Jerusalem carrying the usual image of the emperor on the standards. To the Jews this meant emperor worship and they made violent protest to Pilate in Cæsarea and threw themselves on the ground, preferring death to the violation of their

laws. Pilate only then relented as he had not contemplated wholesale massacre. He outraged the
Jews again by using money from the temple treas-
ury (*corban*) to build aqueducts into Jerusalem
(*Ant.* XVIII. iii. 2). Luke 13:1, tells of some
"Galileans whose blood Pilate mingled with their
sacrifices." Barabbas led a sedition which illustrates the unsettled condition of the country, Mark
15:7. Pilate was finally deposed by Vitellius, Proprætor of Syria, for killing so many Samaritans
in suppressing an uprising over the promise of an
impostor to show on Mount Gerizim the sacred
vessels hidden there by Moses. This false Messiah
was thus the indirect cause of his removal. Vitellius ordered Pilate to proceed to Rome to report
to Tiberius, the Emperor, who died before his ar-
rival. That was March 16, A. D. 37. Pilate was
Procurator of Judea A. D. 26 to 36.

Little is known of his family history. His first
name is not given, only his second name, Pontius
(a famous Samnite name), and his third, Pilatus
(probably "armed with a pike"). He was a Roman
citizen and belonged to the equestrian class. He
probably had military experience. The procurator
was an imperial official and responsible to the emperor. He was subordinate to the Proprætor of
Syria. The Sanhedrin retained many judicial functions, but not the power of life and death which
they once had. The ruler of Judea had to be a man
of some ability and skill, for the Jews were a difficult race to rule. Souter holds that he was "doubtless in many respects a competent governor." But

he failed in his great crisis. Many men can do well when all goes well. But it is the hour of trial which reveals a man's real caliber. Pilate stands convicted as an unjust judge by his own words and by his own conduct. One is reminded of Christ's parable of the judge who feared not God and regarded not man who boasted of his arrogance (Luke 18:2–5). Only this unjust judge did yield to the widow's plea. Pilate, on the other hand, stifled his own sense of justice for political and personal reasons. He went against his own conception of law and right in order to save his place. It seems only retributive justice that he lost it at last because of a false Messiah.

In order to make good this charge against Pilate it is only necessary to make a careful study of the data in the Gospels concerning the trial of Jesus. No one of the Gospels tells all the story. Mark's is the shortest as it is the earliest account. John's narrative is much the fullest and furnishes an easy framework for the details in the Synoptic Gospels. The author of the Fourth Gospel was present during the trial and so had first-hand knowledge of the proceedings. Hence the Fourth Gospel makes plainer what is told in the Synoptics. Those who deny the historical worth of the Fourth Gospel have here something to consider. All the Gospels are used in this picture of Pilate.

When Jesus is brought to Pilate by the Sanhedrin, he naturally asks for a definite charge (John 18:29). They probably tell him that they think him guilty, though there is no indication that the

Sanhedrin told Pilate of the trial and condemnation of Jesus by them. At any rate they make no mention of it. They had condemned Jesus for blasphemy, but they do not refer to that charge at all. They first take a bold stand that they would not have brought Jesus to him if he were not an evildoer (John 18:30). Pilate did not wish to be bothered with petty cases and allowed the Sanhedrin a great deal of latitude anyhow. Hence he said: "Take him yourselves and judge him according to your law" (John 18:31). They had the right to try minor cases. But the Sanhedrin reveal their animus by saying: "It is not lawful for us to put any man to death" (*ib.*). Hence Pilate called for specific accusations. The Sanhedrin make three: a general charge of sedition as a perverter of the nation, forbidding to give tribute to Cæsar, and calling himself Christ a King (Luke 23:2). These charges are all of a political nature and compelled attention at the hands of Pilate. The first is very vague and the second is flatly untrue, for Jesus had seen through the craftiness of the spies sent to trap him on that very point (Luke 20:20–26). The third is true as Jesus means his words, for on oath he had confessed to the Sanhedrin that he was the Christ, the Son of God (Matt. 26:63). But the Sanhedrin condemned Jesus for blasphemy because he claimed to be the Messiah the Son of God, not because he asserted that he was "Christ a King" in the political sense. The Sanhedrin know that Pilate will take the word "king" in a political sense whatever he may think of the epithet "Christ." If he ignores the charge that Jesus sets himself up as a rival to Cæsar, Pilate will be accused before Cæsar and lose his position and probably his life. Cæsar will brook no rival and no rebellion. The Sanhedrin know perfectly well that Jesus makes no such claim though the Triumphant Entry gave them the specious excuse for the charge. The multitude had hailed Jesus as King in the hearing of the Pharisees (Luke 19:30f). A year before in Galilee the crowd had wanted to take Jesus by force and make him king (John 6:14f).

So Pilate was compelled to notice this charge. He took Jesus within the palace and asked him pointedly: "Art thou the King of the Jews?" (John 18:33). The first interview between Pilate and Jesus reveals the weakness and helplessness of Pilate. He does not comprehend a kingdom not of this world, whose citizens will not fight, and which is confined to the realm of truth (John 18:34–38). Pilate feels sure that this peculiar kingdom of truth, whatever it may be, is not in conflict with that of Cæsar. Pilate had probably heard of Jesus before as Herod Antipas had in Galilee, but his own judgement is now clear after this first interview that Jesus is a harmless enthusiast, perhaps erratic, even a bit unbalanced in his devotion to what he called truth, but clearly no rival of Cæsar in any political or legal sense. Hence Pilate steps out of the palace and announces his decision to the Sanhedrin and the multitudes who have now assembled at the beginning of day: "I find no crime in him" (John 18:38; Luke 23:4). In this first phase of the

Roman trial Pilate at least shows no prejudice
against Jesus and renders his decision in accord-
ance with the facts as he finds them, though he is
unable to fathom the mystery of Christ's person
and claims.

The rulers were thunderstruck by this defeat of
their plans of hate and death. They repeated their
accusations with many additions, so that Pilate
turned to Jesus to see if he had anything to say in
reply to their charges (Mark 15:4). But Jesus remained silent to the amazement of Pilate (Matt.
27:14). The rulers saw that the sympathy of Pilate
was with Jesus and that they had to overcome his
first decision. They renew with energy the charge
that Jesus is a disturber of the people all the way
from Galilee to Jerusalem (Luke 23:5).

Pilate now makes his first serious blunder. He
had made his decision, but he lacked the courage to
stand by his conviction of duty towards the prisoner in the face of public clamor. He eagerly seized
a chance to avoid responsibility at the mention of
Galilee. That would throw Jesus under the juris-
diction of Herod Antipas who happened to be in
Jerusalem at that very time. Herod Antipas had
been jealous of Pilate and curious to see Jesus. So
Pilate saw a chance to get rid of a troublesome case
and at the same time please a native ruler who was
hostile to him. It looked like a masterstroke to Pilate in his predicament. He knew that Jesus was
innocent and he did not wish to condemn him, but if
he stuck to his decision already rendered, the Jews
would take it very ill and get him in serious trouble

with Cæsar. With great glee Pilate sent Jesus off
to Herod Antipas (Luke 23:6–12). The Galilean
tetrarch had evidently gotten over his guilty fears
that Jesus was John the Baptist come to life again
(Mark 6:14–29). Now he wanted Jesus to perform
miracles for his entertainment like an oriental
juggler. But the dignified silence of Jesus baffled
Herod and the chief priests and scribes. So Herod
made a mock of Jesus and sent him back to Pilate.
But he and Pilate became friends as a result of the
incident.

Once again Pilate had Jesus on his hands. The
dodge had failed and now Pilate must act. He
seized upon the failure of Herod to condemn Jesus
to defend his previous decision of the innocence of
Jesus which he reaffirmed (Luke 23:13–16). Pilate
boldly announced that he would chastise him and
release him, a sop to Cerberus, for he had no right
to scourge an innocent man, except that Jesus was
not a Roman citizen. In the eyes of Pilate Jesus was
merely a slave with no inherent rights of any kind.
He was more concerned to conform to the forms of
Roman justice and legal jurisprudence than he was
to be merciful or even just to Jesus. Souter reminds
us that "Pilate had a tender enough conscience or
a sound enough idea of justice to try to save this
'slave.'" Yes, but he did not save him. He struggled
with the forces of evil around him and yielded at
last to public clamor and injustice, a thing that a
just judge never does. He had the reins of justice
in his own hands. It was far more important for
justice to be done to a prisoner than for the judge

to retain his office. Pilate bethought him of the custom of releasing a prisoner at the passover. He knew that for envy the rabbis had delivered Jesus to him (Matt. 27:18). He knew also something of the popularity of Jesus with the multitudes. Besides, his wife had sent him a message about a troubled dream that she had had because of Jesus. She warned him to have nothing to do with Jesus (Matt. 27:19). He even dared to call Jesus, "the King of the Jews," as he gave them the choice between Jesus and Barabbas (Mark 15:9). But the chief priests countered this appeal to popular favor by diligent work among the rabble to ask for Barabbas instead of Jesus. Barabbas was himself a sort of hero with a certain element of disorderly disposition. He had led an insurrection and was guilty of murder (Mark 15:7). A successful robber often makes an appeal to the popular imagination. But Pilate pressed the point and demanded which of the two the people wanted to set free. Then with a great shout they all cried out: "Away with this man, and release unto us Barabbas" (Luke 23:18). So Pilate had failed again with this ruse. He had hoped to use the people against the Sanhedrin to justify his release of Jesus.

So once more Pilate has to decide what to do with Jesus. He had Jesus scourged with the hope that this would be enough. He then thought he would get the people into a good humor and make them laugh a bit in the hope that they would still rally to the support of Jesus. So the soldiers arrayed him in a purple garment with a crown of thorns on his head and in mockery hailed him as King of the Jews. Pilate brought Jesus thus be-decked out to the people and said: "Behold, the man" (John 19:5). "What shall I do unto Jesus which is called Christ?" (Matt. 27:22). The people saw no humor in the situation. The chief priests led the shout in reply: "Crucify, crucify him" (Luke 23:21; John 19:6). Pilate argued the matter: "Why, what evil hath this man done? I have found no cause of death in him" (Luke 23:22). But they cried out exceedingly, "Crucify him!" (Mark 15:14). It was now plain to Pilate that he had lost his appeal to the people against the rabbis. It was still his prerogative to stand by his just judgment that Jesus was innocent of any crime. But the pop-ulace had now sided with the Sanhedrin and had made it harder for Pilate to stand up for justice. So in a pet he yielded with a stultifying incrimination of himself: "Take him yourselves and crucify him, for I find no crime in him" (John 19:6). It is im-possible to imagine a more contemptible decision by a judge. In all history it has probably never been surpassed for sheer stupidity. He gave Jesus up to the wolves in order to save his own life. He accused them while excusing himself and asserting the in-nocence of Jesus. But he accused himself also, for he was the judge, not the Sanhedrin, not the mob. His surrender is a travesty upon justice and the acme of judicial cowardice.

The Jews now claim that Jesus ought to die according to their law "because he made himself the Son of God" (John 19:7). This was said to com-

fort the conscience of Pilate who had yielded to the
Jews against the plain dictates of Roman law. But
the description of Jesus as "the Son of God" disturbed Pilate again. He recalled his wife's warning
and the peculiar claim of Jesus about the Kingdom
of Truth. Once more Pilate, moved by his fears,
sought an interview with Jesus (John 19:8–11).
But Jesus was silent at first until Pilate boasted of
his power to release or to crucify Jesus. This boast
convicts Pilate again. He did possess this power
and hence there was no escape from responsibility
and guilt. But, guilty as Pilate was, Judas was
more so.

Once again Pilate came out and sought to release
Jesus, that is, sought to persuade the Jews to be
willing for Pilate to release him. There was never
a moment after the trial began when Pilate could
not have ended the farce by a firm stand. The real
decision was in his own hands. All along Pilate had
been afraid of what now happened. The Jews
bluntly said: "If thou release this man, thou art not
Cæsar's friend; every one that maketh himself a
king speaketh against Cæsar" (John 19:12). The
shadow of this charge had been in the background
all the while. Now it had stepped forth into view.
The hour of final decision had come as Pilate now
knew. It was six o'clock in the morning (John
19:14). The crowd shouted again: "Crucify him!"
Pilate feebly countered, "Shall I crucify your
king?" (John 19:15). The chief priests (Sadducees) now answered: "We have no king but Cæsar."

He had made them confess loyalty to Cæsar at any rate, but he lost his own self-respect and the respect of mankind.

The very effort of Pilate to prove his innocence shows his own consciousness of guilt, washing his hands and saying: "I am innocent of the blood of this righteous man" (Matt. 27:24). The people helped his feeling by saying: "His blood be on us and on our children." It is, alas! There is guilt enough for all of them, for Judas, for the Sanhedrin (Sadducees and Pharisees), for the rabble, for the nation, for Pilate. Each had his share in this crime of the ages.

There is a legend that the body of Pilate after his suicide was finally buried in the territory of Lausanne and that, when heavy storms are on Mount Pilatus, the ghost of Pilate comes out and washes his hands in the vain endeavor to wash out the stain of the blood of Christ. But the stain will never disappear. He knew Roman law and knew that he was violating it in turning over Jesus, an innocent man, to the rage of the Jews. He had his great moral opportunity and fell down before it. It is idle as it is futile to find excuses for his conduct in the scheming of the Sanhedrin and the clamor of the rabble. There are always excuses for crimes. The difference between a man of character and a weakling is precisely this: Let justice be done though the heavens fall. Pilate preferred for justice to be done, provided it did not hurt him. There are too many men in public life like Pilate. They are open to graft, to influence, to patronage, to partisanship. They would rather do right and what is best for the country, but the election is coming and they want votes. Pilate is the unjust judge of all time. He acquitted the innocent prisoner and then turned him over to the rage of the rabble to save his own miserable neck.

CHAPTER VI

THE RICH YOUNG RULER: A YOUNG MAN WHO MISSED THE HIGHEST

(Mark 10:17–31; Matthew 19:16–30; Luke 18:18–30).

THE Rich Young Ruler is an example of the young men to-day who come near the highest things and then fall back to a life of failure.

Some hold that he was Saul of Tarsus, who afterwards came to Christ. According to this view Paul alludes to his previous knowledge of Christ before his conversion in 2 Corinthians 5:16 when he says: "wherefore henceforth we know no one according to the flesh: though we have known Christ according to the flesh, but now no longer do we so know him." A fascinating theory is this which has attracted a number of scholars including the late James Hope Moulton. But the phrase "according to the flesh" (*kata sarka*) naturally means "as the flesh looks at Christ" rather than "Christ in the flesh." Dr. Edward Shillito, of London, is probably correct in the sharp contrast that he draws in an imaginary conversation between Paul and the Ruler, who possibly were schoolmates and met in Rome when Paul was a prisoner for the Christ whom the Young Ruler had rejected. Each looked with pity on the other as their lives had drifted so

63

far apart, but Paul towers far above him. In truth nothing at all is known of him save what the Synoptic Gospels tell us.

There is a great charm in the young man that won the heart of Jesus at first sight. Mark (10:21) records that Jesus fell in love (ingressive aorist tense) with him when He looked upon him for the first time. Jesus looked this young man full in the face, and His heart leaped out toward him. He yearned for him as a disciple and follower. The Rich Young Ruler had come to his hour of destiny.

He was an outstanding youth in his community. He had wealth. He had political office. He had social standing. All these pre-requisites he had, besides the charm of his engaging personality. It is small wonder that he so completely won the heart of Christ. He would win the praise and affection of every lover of the best in human life.

Yet he was not happy. He had great unrest. He knew by the witness of his own heart that he was not perfect as he longed to be. Every young man has a problem. Some have many. Every young man is a problem to his loved ones. It is a pity that it is so difficult to get to the hearts of many young men. The very finest spirits are sometimes so reticent and shy that one cannot penetrate the outer surface.

But this one had heard of Jesus as a wonderful teacher, who understood the ways of the soul. By chance Jesus came his way in His journeys. Here was his great opportunity. He was not going to let it slip. So he came eagerly running and fell on his knees before Jesus. He brought his problem to Jesus instead of concealing it or seeking to forget it. He was sure that Jesus could tell him what to do for his heartache and soul hunger. "Good Teacher, what shall I do that I may get (Matthew), or inherit (Mark and Luke) eternal life?" The *summum bonum* of life was eternal life. All the rabbis taught that. They held out that hope as the price of a life perfect in details, a boon to be bought by obedience to a world of ritual observances. He was willing to do anything within reason to satisfy the ethical demands of his teachers. So he put his problem right up to Jesus. He was not affected or sophisticated. He was sincere and called for serious treatment.

Jesus met him squarely with a challenge. He had greeted Jesus with courtesy that might be mere politeness. "Why do you speak of me as good? No one is absolutely good except God." This reply is not a disclaimer of deity on the part of Christ, but a direct thrust at the young man's real attitude towards Christ himself. "You know the commandments!" "If you wish to enter into life, keep on observing the commandments." Jesus was meeting the young man on his own ground.

"What sort of commandments?"

Jesus reminds him of the outstanding ethical ideals in the Ten Commandments about murder, adultery, theft, false witness, honoring father and mother, with the summary of it all in loving one's neighbor as oneself.

There was disappointment in the reply of the

young ruler who had anticipated some great and
original contribution to rabbinical ethics, on a par
with Hillel's negative form of the Golden Rule.
Each great rabbi made at least one great contribution to the *Torah*. The young man expected
Jesus to make a great deliverance that would
throw the needed light upon his own darkened
soul. Instead of that he had heard only the common-
places of the Mosaic Covenant, upon which he had
been brought up from his mother's knee. "These,
every one of them, I have observed from my youth."
He had learned the *Torah* when a child, these pre-
cepts in particular, and had tried to obey the law,
yet he realized vaguely that something was amiss.
There are parents in plenty who would be intensely
happy if they knew for certain that their sons
knew and lived up to the demands made by the Ten
Commandments. No special code of morals has been
invented for them. The standard for rich and poor
is all the same.

There is sincerity in the cry of the young ruler,
"What lack I yet?" He did not wish to lack anything if he could help it. How near the kingdom of
God this young man seemed to be. He was seeking
Jesus and eternal life at His hands. He was eager
to follow the leadership of Jesus. He was hanging
on the words of the great Teacher who looked on
him intently and fell in love with him. "If you wish
to be perfect, one thing still fails you." Think of
that. This young man lacked only one mark of perfection. His grade in school language would be
ninety-nine. Most young men would be content with

far less than this. Some young men think it not *au fait* to be brilliant in school, diligent in work, or remarkably pious and moral, but this young man wanted the highest within his reach, or thought that he did.

He was in the grip of one of the deadliest sins and did not know it until Jesus turned the flashlight of truth upon his soul. "Go, sell all whatever you have and distribute to poor people, and you will have treasure in heaven. Then come on and follow me all the way." Now the young man had his shock. The mental reaction of the wealthy young man was visible in his countenance, for his face became sad and revealed his utter disappointment in Jesus. He was greatly grieved that Jesus had made this demand of all things on earth.

Without his property he would be as a common day-laborer if not a pauper and a beggar. He took it all in after a moment of intellectual illumination as he faced his opportunity and crisis. He felt sure that Jesus had misjudged him. It was true that he was very rich, but that was no crime. Job had been very wealthy as was King David. Jesus himself had rich disciples, like the Bethany family and later Joseph of Arimathea. The Jews looked on wealth as proof of the favor of God and poverty as a curse. The young man was puzzled beyond expression. The New Teacher had cut across the path of all his training and conviction. He did not know that he was covetous. He probably gave alms regularly. He did not know that he worshiped mammon. Jesus did not mean that no one could be His disciple who

did not first give away all his money. He did not
mean that this was the only sin that could imperil
a man's life. He did not mean that all men were in
the grip of this particular sin of greed. But He
made this stiff test of this particular young man
because he was in reality in the grip of the money-
devil. He was worshiping the almighty dollar.
Many people to-day do not consider covetousness a
vice at all, but rather a virtue. When did you ever
know a man to be excluded from church on the
charge of covetousness? And yet few sins are more
blighting to the soul. The finer traits shrivel up
under the blasting effect of the exaggerated love of
money. Jesus evidently means the young man who
posed so near perfection to see that he had violated
the very first of the Ten Commandments. He loved
money more than he did God. There are many com-
placent church members to-day who would receive
a severe jolt if they realized that they actually
loved money more than they did the cause of Christ.
The preacher to-day is placed in an embarrassing
position about money. If he exposes the "skin-
flints" for their stinginess, they will try to make
him resign or at least criticize him for always talking about money instead of preaching the simple
gospel of grace which they conceive to be devoid of
any financial obligations. A pastor should be faithful in exposing the sin of covetousness and in warning men of the peril to the soul in the love of gold
with its grasping greed.

Jesus promised the rich young ruler treasure in
heaven if he would break the power of money over

his own life. Each of the Synoptic Gospels pre-
serves this item. Jesus used the same figure elsewhere, as in Matthew 6. The word for treasure
(thesaurus) we have preserved in our English. To
have treasure in heaven is an appealing figure. We
can lay up treasure in heaven by the right use of
our money here. The only way to take money to
heaven is to give it away here.

Jesus demanded the surrender of all his wealth.
Jesus wanted no half-hearted service from this
gifted young man. He demanded his whole heart, his
whole life, his whole wealth. The young man was
called on to lay all upon the altar. "Then come and
go on following me," said Jesus. "Follow me all
the time and all the way to baptism, to the cross."
It was the call to the high and the heroic. That appeal has always found a prompt and enthusiastic
response from young men through all the ages. But
it meets a loyal acceptance from those who have
come to Christ and who have left self behind. This
one had come to Christ for advice and was willing
to pay any reasonable price for the eternal life that
he so much desired. He would probably have agreed
to go on a long pilgrimage to some sacred place, to
live a life of abstemiousness for some considerable
time, to fast and to pray, to pay a good deal of
money by way of alms or for kingdom work. He
was undoubtedly prepared to do much and to meet
Jesus half way. But he was not ready to go the
whole way and to put all at the service of Christ
even to win so great a prize as eternal life. Jesus
demanded that there be no private reservations, no

secret places in the heart reserved for self, no exceptions in what he gave up. It was a drastic demand that searched the inmost recesses of the young man's life. He was willing to give up all the sins of which he was not guilty. He only hesitated about this one sin which he had thought was a virtue, this one defect in his life which kept him back from perfection. Beyond a doubt many a man is held back from the service of Christ because he is unwilling to give up the pet sin or sins which he hugs closely to his heart. It often happens that such a man talks much about the intellectual difficulties in Christianity, about the things that he cannot understand and cannot believe, about the doubts raised by scientists or by theologians and what not. At bottom they are all excuses to hide the secret or open sin in his own life.

An hour before this young man had come running up to Jesus with all deference. Now, with a broken and disappointed heart he turned away from Jesus and went back to his money and to his life of selfishness. He was saddened beyond words that Jesus had made such an impossible demand. There are people to-day who say that Christianity must be toned down to meet the views of the modern "youth movement," that university men and women to-day will not have the Jesus of theology and will put up only with the Jesus of history, a mere man at that, who will condone the life of "modern" men and who will not make demands of young people of culture and enlightenment to which they will not accede. Jesus to-day meets a threat from certain self-appointed leaders who defiantly proclaim that they will not follow Jesus "unless." But to-day, as when the Rich Young Ruler rejected Jesus, it is impossible to conceive of Jesus as granting "ifs" in order to win the nominal service of young people of wealth and culture. Jesus Christ asks for all or for nothing. He asks for the whole of life. He does not ask that we stop thinking, but that we think rightly. Our age greatly needs the warning of this brilliant young man.

He went away from Christ and, so far as we know, he never came back. He made the final, the irrevocable choice. He chose his life of ease and pleasure to the consecration demanded by Jesus. One thinks of Saul of Tarsus who was challenged on the road to Damascus and gave up all for Christ and who became the great Apostle to the Gentiles. Paul became poor and made many rich. The Rich Young Ruler met his crisis and missed his greatest opportunity in life.

There is the sad reflection that Jesus Himself, the Saviour of sinners, failed to save this young man whom He loved so much. As the Physician of souls, Jesus diagnosed the young man's case rightly. He put his finger on the sore spot, but the young man refused to submit to the operation. We come up against the age-long problem of divine sovereignty and human free agency. There is nothing new to say about it. God has to be sovereign else He is not God. Man has to be free else he is not a free moral agent. But God respects the rights of the individual and his personality. In the last analysis, if a man wills to serve the worst and to be the slave of sin, he can so decide.

It is not surprising that preachers to-day sometimes fail to win young men of the highest promise. We make mistakes ourselves and do not possess the consummate wisdom and power of Jesus in winning souls. And then we strike the same hardness of heart that had this young ruler in its grip. But it is a tragedy, whenever it happens, to see so fine a man lost to the highest and the best.

Christ's failure to win the young man deeply moved his own soul. He looked around (Mark) and said to the disciples, after the young man had gone: "With how much difficulty do those who have wealth enter the kingdom of God." The disciples were doubtless saddened also by the choice of the young man. But the saying of Jesus surprised them, for the Jews regarded money as a mark of divine favor and not a hindrance to the life of faith. Jesus explained: "It is easier for a camel to go through the eye of a needle (surgeon's needle, Luke says) than for a rich man to enter the kingdom of God." This illustration depressed them still more. "Who then can be saved?" The thing looked hopeless for all. Then Jesus looked on the disciples again in pity and admitted that it was impossible with men, but added that God can do the impossible. God can save a rich man just like any other sinner. Peter added the naïve remark that they had left all to follow Christ, which was quite true. Each of the Twelve Apostles had given up his business in order to follow Christ. In some cases there may have been opposition in the home circle. Jesus appreciates to the full the sacrifices that they had made and promises fullness of blessings in this life "along with persecutions" and in the coming age eternal life. It was a solemn time of testing as Jesus added: "Many first ones will be last and many last ones will be first."

CHAPTER VII

MARY MAGDALENE THE MISREPRESENTED WOMAN

GET a misunderstanding started and it is almost impossible to stop it. Correction never overtakes the original slander. There is absolutely nothing in the records of the Gospels as ground for the notion that Mary Magdalene was a harlot who was won to Christ. There are real objections to that view which will be stated later.

The worst form of the slander involves Christ also and pictures Mary Magdalene as the paramour of Jesus. It is difficult to be patient or to be courteous towards one who offers a slur upon the character of Christ. Evil to him who evil thinks. Certainly Jesus needs no defense from this slander, nor does Mary, but she has been attacked in so many ways that it is only fair to her memory to answer the slanders. No one doubts the power of Christ to rescue and to change a woman of evil life. He has done it time and again with women and men and he can work that miracle of grace to-day. But the possession of this power is no proof that it was actual fact in the case of Mary Magdalene.

One of the later legends says not simply that Mary Magdalene had been a harlot, but relapsed into her former mode of life and "abused all her admirable gifts to tempt others to sin" (J. B. Mayor, Hasting's *Dictionary of the Bible*). This late legend is even worse than the way some articles have treated her as the synonym of the repentant and converted harlot so that the very name *Magdalene* to-day has come to carry that meaning. The name is now applied to houses of reform for fallen women. It is too late to change the current of actual usage, but we can at least be free from the sin of misrepresenting so noble a woman as Mary Magdalene.

Let us trace the story. The name "Magdalene" is probably due to her coming from Magdala (or Magadan of Matt. 15:39), a town some three miles from Capernaum at the southern end of the Plain of Genneseret. All that the epithet means is that she was Mary of Magdala, or Mary the Magdalene, to distinguish her from the other Marys. Several rabbis in the Talmud are termed Magdalene. There is the ruin of a miserable village to-day called *Mejdel*. Tristran (*Bible Places,* p. 260) says "Magdala is only the Greek form of *Mighdol* or watchtower, one of the many places of the name in Palestine." The ancient Magdala was a wealthy city and the Talmud says that its tribute had to be carried to Jerusalem in wagons. The town had a bad reputation, like Corinth, and the rabbis gave this as the cause for its final destruction. It was celebrated for its dye works and was a Sabbath day's journey from Tiberias. But it is folly to translate the term Magdalene the same as harlot. How about the rabbis called Magdalene?

Some of the rabbis say that Magdalene means a plaiter of hair and that women of loose character made a point of wearing long plaited hair like the sinful woman who wiped her tears from the feet of Jesus with her hair (Luke 7:38). Surely this is a fanciful reason for maligning the character of Mary.

It is argued also by some that Mary Magdalene had seven demons cast out of her, which proves that she had been a woman of evil life. Jerome (*Vit. Hil. Erem*) does speak of a *Virgo Dei* at Majumas as possessed of *amoris daemon*. Some of the Jews did consider demoniac possession as involving immorality, probably true of some, but it is a large jump to conclude that therefore it was true of Mary. Jesus spoke of the man from whom a demon was cast out and into whom the demon came again with seven other demons worse than the first, so that the last state of that man was worse than the first (Matt. 12:45—Luke 11:26), but it is a leap in logic to conclude that therefore this was true of Mary and that she had a sevenfold possession of passion instead of a sevenfold endowment of grace. The one possessed of a demon was regarded and treated by Jesus as the victim of the evil spirit, not as an accomplice in vice. Jesus did not blame these victims for their sad condition. The divided consciousness, peculiar frenzy, and long fits of silence of the demoniac make it wholly unlikely that Mary was a harlot. Her condition was bad enough. Recall the case of the wild man who had two thousand demons in him and how uncontrollable he was before he was healed. Surely Mary Magdalene had grounds enough for deep gratitude to Jesus.

Those who treat Mary Magdalene as an abandoned woman identify her with the woman of the street who slipped into the house of Simon the Pharisee with an alabaster box of myrrh and stood at the feet of Jesus, weeping, who wet his feet with her tears and wiped them with her hair, who kissed his feet and anointed them with the myrrh. There is no question concerning the character of this woman. She was a woman of the town and the pious Pharisee was amazed that Jesus, passing as a prophet, should be so ignorant as to allow such a woman to take liberties of this nature (Luke 7:39). But Jesus did know of her many sins and had forgiven her. Her great love was due to the forgiveness she had received. Was she Mary Magdalene? If so, why did not Luke say so? It is hardly conceivable that Luke would have concealed the name of the sinful woman in chapter 7:35-50 and then adroitly introduced Mary Magdalene in 8:1-3 either to keep his readers from identifying her with the sinful woman or to suggest by inference that she was. Either alternative is quite out of harmony with Luke's method and manner. Of course, Luke may not have known of the evil life if that were a fact, but the Fourth Gospel does not give the slightest indication of such a past life. The introduction of Mary Magdalene in Luke 8:1-3 is plainly that of a new character with no connection with the sinful woman of the preceding paragraph. Mayor says that Luke could easily have said in defense of Jesus

that the sinful woman had been under Satanic influence and freed of demons and hence was showing
her gratitude. But she is simply termed a sinner.
If Mary Magdalene had been a common harlot,
would she have been allowed to travel with Jesus
and his company? Mayor asks if it would not have
been placing an additional temptation in the path
of one known to be unusually weak. If the Messiah
were known to allow one of notorious character to
travel in his group over Galilee, some might draw
wrong conclusions about them all. Luke probably
did not know the name of the sinful woman and
closes the incident about her at the end of chapter 7. Mary Magdalene was "a healed invalid, not a
rescued social derelict" (L. M. Sweet). We do not
find that Mary Magdalene did anoint the feet of
Jesus. She is introduced in Luke 8:2 as a new character with no connection with the sinful woman
at all.

Let Mary stand upon her own feet in the group
of women in Luke 8:1–3. This is a notable company, the first organization of women for the support of the gospel of Christ. What would have been
the fate of Christianity if it had appealed only to
men like Mithraism, its chief rival in the second
and third centuries? These women had all been
healed of various diseases and had particular
grounds for gratitude to Jesus. They were minister-
ing with their property for the support of Jesus
and his group of twelve preachers. It required
courage and circumspection for these women to
carry out this laudable enterprise and they prob-

ably incurred criticism. Apparently they had all
been healed of evil spirits and weaknesses, but
Mary Magdalene had special occasion for consecration because seven demons had gone out of her. The
number of women is not given, though Luke says
that they were "many." Blessings on these women
who were the first to rally to the call of Christ for
money.

Legend goes further with Mary Magdalene and
actually identifies her with Mary of Bethany as
well as with the sinful woman of Luke 7 and on
even less basis of fact. It is argued that the name
of the host in each of the two anointings is Simon,
but this was a very common name. In one case it is
Simon the Pharisee who sneers at Jesus, his guest.
In the other case it is Simon the leper who gives a
feast in honor of Jesus. The one anointing is by a
woman who had been a sinner, the other by Mary
of Bethany, who does it with her mind on the death
of Jesus. She alone showed any comprehension of
that tragic event coming upon them. The Pharisee's
complaint is about the ignorance of Jesus. The
other complaint is about the wastefulness of Mary
of Bethany. A mere detail is that in both cases there
is an anointing and wiping of the feet of Jesus with
the hair. Clearly Luke does not describe Mary
Magdalene in Chapter 7 under the guise of a sinful
woman, for he introduces her as a new character
in 8 :2. Least of all does he mean in 10 :38–42 that
Mary of Bethany is Mary Magdalene and certainly
not the sinful woman of Chapter 7. Martha and
Mary, her sister, are given their first description by

Luke in 10:38–42. The Mary of Bethany here bears no similarity at all to Mary Magdalene. Luke alone, in chapter 7, gives the anointing apparently during the Galilean ministry while Matthew and Mark and John give the one at the close of the ministry during passion week. It is only by a patient examination of all the confusion created by legend in the light of actual Scriptural data that one can sweep aside the cobwebs spun through the centuries. All three of these women had abundant cause for gratitude to Christ, but that does not mean identification. Legions of other women were also grateful. It is impossible to think that John in the Fourth Gospel confused Mary of Bethany and Mary Magdalene, either from ignorance or on purpose. It is hard, besides, to think of Mary Magdalene as the sister of Martha.

There seems to be no end of speculative confusion in ancient writings. One tries to identify Mary Magdalene as the daughter of the Syro-Phœnician woman. Another suggests that there were two Mary Magdalenes, one in Matthew and the other in John. Baring-Gould suggests that the starting point of most of these legends is due to the traditions about Marius who defeated the Ambrons and Teutons at Aix B. C. 102. At Les Baux where Marius encamped, an ancient sculpture of three figures is called *Tremaie* which Gilles interprets as Marius, his wife, Julia, and the prophetess Martha. But tradition has taken this to include Mary Magdalene. There is another *Trois Maries* sculpture at

Camargue. So legend grows spinning out fanciful details.

Mary Magdalene is a clear-cut figure in the Gospels, if painters would only take her as she is there depicted. She does not appear again in the narrative till we see her standing at the Cross of Jesus with the mother of Jesus, her sister, and Mary, the wife of Cleopas. She was one of the watchers of the Cross. The mother of Jesus was taken away from the Cross to the home of the Beloved Disciple (John 19:26–27), but the other women ("many other women") remained "beholding from afar" (Mark 15:40) the dreadful tragedy, these faithful women who had followed Jesus all the way from Galilee (Matt. 27:56; Luke 23:49). These women were at the Cross when all the apostles but John had fled in terror. The other of the sons of Zebedee was there, but John and James were not there. Mary Magdalene was apparently the leader of this group of women in the sad vigil at the Cross of Christ.

When Jesus was really dead, "Mary Magdalene and Mary, the mother of Jesus, beheld where he was laid" (Mark 15:47). Mark uses the imperfect tense (*etheoroun*) and it was therefore more than a casual glance, a prolonged and anxious watch as Mary Magdalene and the other Mary were "sitting over against the tomb" (Matthew 27:61). They observed how his body was "laid" (Luke 23:55) and then returned and rested during the Sabbath day (Luke 23:56). It was a sad and sorrowful Sabbath. Somehow the women managed to go through the gloom of that dark day. The women apparently knew nothing of the Roman guard which Pilate had put at the tomb.

Late on the Sabbath day Mary Magdalene and the other Mary went to see the sepulcher (Matthew 28:1; Luke 23:56). After the Sabbath was over (at sundown) Mary Magdalene and Mary, the mother of James and Salome, bought spices, that they might anoint him (Mark 16:1). Then they waited till next morning while it was yet dark and Mary Magdalene and the other women started from Bethany with the spices. When they reached the tomb to the north of Jerusalem, the sun had risen (John 20:1; Luke 24:1; Mark 16:2). According to John's account, Mary Magdalene ran in her eagerness and arrived at the tomb before the rest. She stopped long enough to see that the stone was rolled away, without looking into the tomb. She draws the conclusion that there had been a grave robbery. She suspects the enemies of Christ of having done this despicable thing. At any rate it was clearly a man's job. Mary Magdalene hurries on without waiting for the other women to tell Peter and John her fears: "They have taken away the Lord out of the tomb, and we know not where they have laid him." She was mistaken in her interpretation of the empty tomb, but it was a natural error. She followed on after Peter and John and arrived after they had departed.

Mark, in the disputed close of the Gospel (16:9), says that Jesus "appeared first to Mary Magdalene

from whom he had cast out seven demons." This
testimony, though probably not a part of Mark's
Gospel, yet has the confirmation of John's Gospel.
Some critics wish to discredit this first witness to
the resurrection of Jesus. It is urged that she was a
paranoiac and was in the habit of seeing things.
Because of her previous condition at the hands of
the demons she is pictured as a nervous wreck. Certainly she does not act then as if she was a victim
of tremors and hallucinations. She did not expect
the resurrection of Jesus from the dead and she
does not imagine that fact as the explanation of
the empty tomb. She was the last at the Cross and
the first at the tomb and shows keen interest in the
empty tomb as a probable desecration. Her witness
does not come from a woman who is a nervous
wreck.

John's Gospel (20:11–19) gives the marvelous
picture of Mary in her interview with the risen
Christ. She was standing outside weeping as she
paused a moment before looking into the tomb.
Peter and John had gone and Mary knew nothing
of John's intuitive conclusion that the Lord was
risen (John 20:8). She finally stooped and looked
through her tears into the empty tomb. Amazed
she saw two angels in the tomb, clad in white, sitting one at the head and the other at the foot. For
some reason Peter and John did not see these angels, though the other women had seen them (Mark
16:5–8; Matt. 28: 5–8; Luke 24:4–8). Luke speaks
of "two men," while Mark mentions only one
"young man sitting on the right side." Matthew

calls this *man* an *angel*. It is not pertinent therefore to say that Mary Magdalene just imagined
that she saw the angels. What about the other
women? Mary Magdalene knew nothing at all of
their experience. Mary Magdalene told the same
story to the angels that she had given to Peter and
John. Her fear was that enemies of Christ had
robbed the grave of the body of Jesus.

Why did Mary Magdalene turn back at this juncture? Her eyes were full of blinding tears and not
expecting to see Jesus, the Risen Christ. In the case
of Cleopas and his companion their eyes were
holden so that they did not recognize Jesus (Luke
24:16). Mark has it that Jesus appeared in "another form" (16:12). At any rate Mary has a new
idea no more right than the other one. She suspects
that the gardener has merely moved the body of
Jesus to another tomb for a fresh burial in this
tomb. There is the utmost pathos and tenderness in
her words: "Sir, if thou hast borne him hence, tell
me where thou hast laid him, and I will take him
away." Her mind is still all bent on honoring the
body of Jesus with no hope of his resurrection. That
was her reply to the question of Jesus: "Woman,
why weepest thou? Whom seekest thou?" There is
no indication of the sudden revelation that came to
Mary Magdalene first of all. It came clearly from
no psychological peculiarity of Mary Magdalene.
Her mind was all turned in another direction.

In moments of great tragedy, of sorrow, of joy,
one can say very little. Words come with difficulty
and fail to express the deep emotion felt. Jesus said

simply, "Mariam" as the Greek has it, the Aramaic form of the name. He spoke it with the accent that she knew and loved. There was no mistaking his voice, now that she saw with undimmed eyes. Her mind was no longer holden and Jesus was not in another form. When he stood before her, her theories of grave robbery and then of the removal of the body by the gardener vanished like mist before the sun. And yet what can she say? There was only one word to utter. It was "Rabboni," likewise in Aramaic, "My Lord," "My Rabbi," "My Master." This word told it all. Mary Magdalene confronted the Risen Christ with dignity, with faith, with joy.

Mary Magdalene did not restrain a natural impulse to take hold of Jesus, to put her hands upon him, to cling to him in joy. But this was going too far. Jesus did allow the other women to clasp his feet as they worshiped him (Matthew 28:9). So he said to Mary Magdalene, "Cease clinging to me." He explains why he is still here: "For I am not yet ascended to the Father." It is not as it once was and his body is in a transition state before he is glorified. Probably Mary Magdalene could not comprehend this clearly, though she did not demur.

But Jesus had a message for Mary to carry to the brethren: "Say to them, I ascend unto my Father and your Father, and my God and your God." He has brought a new conception of God as Father and now he links the disciples with him in the glorious fellowship. It is the Son of God in a sense not true of others, but Jesus calls us his *brothers* with the same Father, God.

It was a message of mystery and of joy. Mary Magdalene added some words of her own as she told it. It was the most wonderful message ever brought by merely human lips, "I have seen the Lord." This was her crown of glory. It should have brought untold joy to all, but they were not ready to believe Mary's story. They "disbelieved" her (Mark 16:11), possibly thinking Mary had the demons back again. They were mourning and weeping (Mark 16:10), but the talk of the women was "idle talk" (Luke 24:10, 22).

Mary Magdalene's story was confirmed by that of Simon Peter (Luke 24:34; I Corinthians 15:5) and that brought conviction. But she was right before Simon Peter bore his witness. John has evidently taken joy in painting the noble picture of Mary Magdalene as she carried the glad news of the Risen Lord. She is the first herald of the Gospel of the Risen Christ, the message that has brought cheer to the world.

CHAPTER VIII

Epaphras the Newsbearer

News is one of the most important things in the world. The great newspaper world rests upon the promulgation of news. Many a man has to decide what is news before he puts it in his papers. The taste of the public about daily, weekly, monthly, and quarterly journals, is whimsical and changing. Even the government has to place limits on the circulation of certain kinds of journals, yellow and rotten. In Athens when Paul was there, he found the fidgety whimsical fever for the very latest items of news. But all the same the gospel in Greek is good news, the news of salvation, the glad tidings of God's love to men in Christ. The Greek word for preacher is "herald" and the real preacher finds his joy in telling the story of Jesus to men. The peril of the present-day preacher is that he tells the old story in a hum-drum way so that the news element vanishes. That is the great opportunity of the missionary that he has people before him who have not become tired of the message, who may not have heard it before. Kanamori of Japan will not let people hear his three-hour sermon who have heard it before. He tries to tell the whole gospel in one sermon. We cannot do that to-day, but it is within

one's power to make what we do tell fresh and gripping and winning.

Epaphras came to Paul in Rome from Colossae,
where he lived and worked, "Epaphras, who is one
of you" (Col. 4:2). We do not know whether Epaphras was born in Colossae or not, but certainly he
came from that city to Rome. His name is a short-
ened form of Epaphroditus, but he is certainly not
the Epaphroditus from Philippi (Phil. 2:25). It
was common then, as now, for men to have similar
names.

Paul had not visited Colossae (Col. 2:1). It is
probable that Epaphras had heard Paul in Ephesus
or that Paul's message had been carried over Asia
to Epaphras by those who heard Paul in Ephesus.
Paul had said to the elders of Ephesus that for
three years night and day he was in Asia and was
with them all the time (Acts 20:18, 31). He may
have made brief excursions into the province of
Asia, but that is not the natural meaning of Luke's
report. And yet Luke says that both Jews and
Greeks in all Asia heard the word of the Lord
(Acts 19:10) and Demetrius told his fellow-crafts-
men that "almost throughout all Asia this Paul had
persuaded and turned away much people" (Acts
19:26). It seems plain therefore that, directly or
indirectly, Epaphras was a convert from Paul's
work in Ephesus.

But he was more than that. The correct text in
Col. 1:17 speaks of Epaphras as "a faithful minister
of Christ on our behalf" instead of "on your behalf." This is the reading of the oldest Greek manu-

scripts and is clearly correct. So then the meaning is that Epaphras was Paul's representative in Christ, his delegate in the gospel since he could not go himself. Paul while in Ephesus had sent Epaphras to evangelize Colossae as well as Laodicea and Hieropolis (Col. 4:12 and 13), in a word the Lycus Valley. Epaphras had labored much and successfully in this important region of Asia and Paul had great agony of heart about them (Col. 2:1). They had not seen his face, but he had sent Epaphras to them and Paul is grateful for God's blessing on his work. The correct text in Colossians 1:7 makes it plain that Epaphras was the first missionary to them, "even as ye learned from Epaphras." The word "also" is not genuine. Epaphras did not just add to what they already knew as "also" would imply and as is true of most preachers from the nature of the case. He was the very first to tell the story of Christ in this great valley. He was the missionary who was the instrument in winning these people to Christ.

And he did his work well. Paul calls him "our beloved fellow servant" and "faithful minister of Christ" (Col. 1:7). He was an exponent of Paul's gospel and a faithful interpreter of Christ to these important cities in the Lycus Valley. The very zeal of Epaphras for Christ and his strong love for Paul led him to come to Rome to tell the great Apostle to the Gentiles the story of conditions in Asia. Epaphras had done what he could to stem the tide of false teaching that swept into this region. Paul at Miletus had told the Ephesian elders of the grievous wolves that would cause havoc after he had gone (Acts 20:29). So Epaphras goes to Rome to tell Paul, prisoner as he was, the sad situation in Colossae. Men called Gnostics had come who were misleading some of the followers of Christ by their subtle philosophy and affectation of superior learning. These men had a theory of matter as wholly evil and so they held that God could not be the Creator of evil matter. Hence they postulated the hypothesis of *œons* or intermediate agencies that came in below God until one was found far enough away from God to create matter without contaminating God and yet with power enough to do the work. If one wonders at such philosophic foolishness having a following, he has only to recall theosophy to-day and "new thought" and so-called "Christian Science" to understand how gullible some people are. This Gnostic view of creation came in from Persia with a dash of Essenism and confronted Christianity with its Christ. At once some of them said that Christ was one of the lower *œons*. That degrading view of Christ alarmed Epaphras and it alarmed Paul, who wrote the powerful little Epistle to the Colossians to magnify the Headship of Christ in the realm of nature and of grace. Epaphras bore this sad news to Paul and he told it to Paul in such intelligent fashion that Paul grasped the whole situation and expounded the emptiness of this false philosophy and the peril to the faith and lives of these who fell under the spell of these who became either ascetics or libertines. It is a credit to the intelligence and the courage of

Epaphras that he voluntarily turned to Paul as the only man who could handle this great issue.

So Epaphras came to Rome and apparently fell a victim to the Roman hostility to Paul. He calls him "our beloved fellow-bondsman" (Col. 1:7) and "my fellow-captive in Christ Jesus" (Philemon 23). It is possible to take these phrases in a metaphorical sense, but the latter phrase is far more naturally understood in a literal sense. It is used of Aristarchus (Col. 4:10) and of Andronicus and Junias (Rom. 16:7). Paul calls Timothy a "bond-servant of Christ Jesus" (Phil. 1:1) and elsewhere save in Col. 1:7 only of himself. It seems more likely that Epaphras showed so much eagerness to be with Paul that he incurred the displeasure of the authorities in spite of Paul's liberty to see his friends (Acts 28:30) or perhaps he voluntarily assumed captivity with Paul as Aristarchus may have done in order to be with Paul the more constantly. At any rate he was not the bearer of the letter to the Colossians as would have otherwise been the case. He was apparently a sharer of Paul's imprisonment.

Epaphras had by no means lost his interest in the saints in the Lycus Valley. He had given Paul a most favorable report of the progress and faith of the churches there which stirred Paul's heart to gratitude and thanksgiving when he heard it (Col. 1:4-9). Epaphras had told of their faith and love and hope and grasp of the word of truth. The story of Epaphras made Paul pray with renewed zeal that they might have full knowledge of Christ

as an antidote to the false and superficial teachings
of the Gnostics. But Epaphras himself kept up his
agonizing prayer for the Colossians that they may
stand firm and be fully established in the will of
God. So Paul includes the salutation of Epaphras
as the one who has done most for them as disciples
of Christ and who deserves most at their hands
(Col. 4:12 and 13).

So we may think of Epaphras a prisoner with
Paul left behind in Rome while Tychicus and
Onesimus the converted runaway slave bear the
letters to Philemon in Colossae (Col. 4:7–9) and
another circular letter to Hierapolis (Col. 4:16)
which we now call the Epistle to the Ephesians.
Onesimus comes with some embarrassment because
of uncertainty as to what the attitude of Philemon
will be toward Onesimus. Paul throws his whole
heart into the plea to Philemon that must have won
acquiescence. But Tychicus was unhampered. He
will tell the whole story about Paul's situation in
Rome (Col. 4:7). Paul has sent Tychicus for this
very purpose that the Colossians may get fresh
information in fuller form than Paul can put into a
letter. Tychicus will comfort their hearts by the
way that he gives the probabilities about Paul's release. He asked Philemon to reserve a room for him
(Philemon 22). Let us hope that after his release
he did reach Colossae and saw Philemon, but this
is all speculation.

But the Colossians would wish to know also
something about Epaphras. Tychicus could tell
them why he was not able to come back and speak

for himself. He would be sure to tell of his loyalty to the Colossians and how nobly he had presented the whole case of their faith and of the peril in which they were because of the Gnostics. Epaphras had been a wise and faithful interpreter to Paul of the conditions in the Lycus Valley. They were fortunate in having such a man as Epaphras as their minister and now as their pleader with Paul. Their case was in good hands.

We are not able to follow the story of Epaphras any further. There is a tradition that he did return to Colossae and become bishop of the church there. Another tradition is that he suffered martyrdom and that his bones were buried in the church of Sta. Maria Maggiore in Rome. One can only hope that the Colossians did see again the face of this faithful servant of Christ and that Paul also carried out his wish to come. But a veil of silence rests on all this as also on the question whether John Mark ever reached Colossae or not (Col. 4:10). At any rate Paul had sent to the Colossians, probably by Mark himself, a note of kindly commendation. Mark is now in Rome with Paul and sends his greetings with the rest. Epaphras disappears from our knowledge, but he did his work. He was the bearer of good news to the Lycus Valley and to Paul. So let us to-day pass on the glad tidings of Jesus our Lord and Savior.

CHAPTER IX

THE SAMARITAN WOMAN WHO STARTED A REVIVAL

THIS nameless woman is not the only woman who has started a revival of religion. There was Lydia, the first European convert in Paul's ministry, whose conversion led to the founding of the first church in Macedonia, and under Lydia's influence it became the first church that gave financial support to Paul's missionary campaign. It is a great mistake to think women have only of late been active in Christian work. Many a revival through all the centuries has been due to the consecration, prayer, and work of a single woman, sometimes a woman on a bed of affliction who kept in touch with the throne of God.

In the case of the Samaritan woman (John 4:5–42) there were apparently insuperable difficulties in the way of anything that she could do to help on the Kingdom of God. Race prejudice was bitter between the Jews and the Samaritans. The Jews hated the Samaritans all the more because they were half-Jews just as some people to-day give an added touch of dislike to neighbors who are kin to them. Later James and John wanted to call down fire from heaven to consume the Samaritans who did not welcome them when they were going towards Jerusalem (Luke 9:51–56). This woman is greatly surprised that Jesus should rise above this hatred and ask a favor of her, a Samaritan. It is a tragedy to-day that race prejudice and national jealousy play so large a part in the life of nations and of individuals. The Christian leaven of love has not permeated modern life to such an extent that men will usually be just to those of another race or nation.

But this Samaritan was a woman besides being a Samaritan. She felt a sense of inferiority on both grounds and she herself spoke of these two obstacles (John 4:9). The Jews showed their dislike of her as a Samaritan. And men (both Jews and Samaritans) reminded her that she was only a woman. One of the prayers of the rabbis preserved to us was an expression of gratitude to God that the rabbi was not a woman. Even the disciples were astonished (continued to be amazed, imperfect tense *ethaumazon*) that the Master was talking with a woman (John 4:27) in public where anybody could see him. It was not considered good form for a rabbi to speak with a woman in public. It was actually said by rabbis that a husband would be sure of *gehenna* if he talked too much with his wife. And yet the disciples did not dare to ask Jesus why he had not conformed to this convention, much as they wished to do so. All the liberty that women enjoy to-day they owe to Jesus who broke the shackles of bondage by which they were bound.

This woman at first failed to understand the

parable of water, quick as she was in wit and
repartee. Jesus met her on the common ground of
the water from Jacob's well which she had come
to draw at the evening hour (6 P. M., Roman time
used in John's Gospel). He was weary from the
day's journey and was sitting on the curbstone
of the well when the woman came up. Jesus asked
for a drink of water from the well, but, woman
that she was, she had to have the independence of
Jesus explained in his asking a favor of her. But
he quickly changed the topic and affirmed that
she would have asked him for living water, if
she had really known the gift of God. She states
her difficulties, of course, in the way of her understanding this Jewish stranger. He had no bucket
and no rope and the well was deep. Surely he
did not claim (*me,* expecting a negative answer)
to be greater than Jacob who gave them the well.
But Jesus is patient with this woman and explains
that she will never thirst again, but there will be
in her a fountain of water bubbling up into eternal life. Imagine the woman's keen interest in
spite of her apparent dullness about spiritual
things. The metaphor of Jesus was still too deep
for her. Still she bantered back to Jesus that he
would please give her this kind of water that she
might not have to come every evening to this well
and draw the water for her family. The woman is
still the water carrier in the Orient.

Many a preacher has quit when he finds one so
dense as this woman, but Jesus persevered. He
gave her a sudden personal thrust: "Go call your

husband and come here." Clearly she was now em-
barrassed at this unexpected turn of the conversation with this stranger. She was reluctant to heed
his request for it involved exposure of her own life
and there was no telling what this stranger would
say when the two were together before Jesus. Perhaps she felt that her husband would be no match
for this stranger. So she countered by a technical
splitting of hairs as a dodge: "Sir, I have no husband." She thought perhaps that this hedge would
protect her against any further probing of her own
life which she did not wish to discuss. Imagine her
surprise when Jesus bluntly said to her. "You said
well 'I have no husband,' because you have had five
husbands, and now the one that you have is not
your husband. This is strictly true what you have
said." The woman was amazed again at the insight
of the stranger into her own wicked life. But she
has one more line of defense, one that many sinners have tried when the preacher becomes personal and touches a sore spot. She shows a sudden
interest in theology and wants to change the subject to the old dispute between the Jews and Samaritans about the true place to worship God.
She confesses that the stranger is a prophet, meaning this as a compliment, and seizes upon this dis-
covery as her way of escape from further personal
inquiries of an embarrassing nature. The Jews had
their temple in Jerusalem, still wonderful in its
glory. The Samaritans had lost their temple on
Mt. Gerizim which rose majestically above, as she
spoke. But the Samaritans clung to this mountain,

as the handful of them do yet, as the only place
where God should be worshiped. So the woman
with quick repartee raises this famous theological
problem with a sigh of relief. But it was of short
duration, for Jesus explains to her that God is
spiritual and is not confined to one temple or one
mountain and must be worshiped in spirit by men
wherever they are. Jesus definitely, however, said
that salvation was of the Jews.

The woman probably had a sense of weariness
and of disappointment as she replied: "I know
that Messiah comes, who is called Christ. Whenever that one comes he will announce all things
to us." She loses her sudden interest in theology
and falls back upon the Messianic expectations
common to both Jews and Samaritans. The episode would probably have ended right here but
for the startling words of Jesus: "I am he, the
one who is speaking to you." It was like a bolt
out of the blue and gave the woman an electric
shock that precipitated all the previous talk to an
inevitable conclusion. It was now plain that she
was face to face with the long-looked for Messiah
of whose actual advent she had apparently heard
nothing. This was the first appearance of Jesus in
Samaria though John the Baptist had labored in
Aenon near to Salem. The time for decision had
come to this woman and she quickly made up her
mind what to do. It often happens that at critical
moments interruptions come which are sometimes
deplorable in their results. It might have been so
at this time when the disciples came back from

Sychar and found Jesus talking in public with a woman. They evidently showed their surprise to the woman, though they said nothing to Jesus about her.

So she instantly left her water pot and went hurriedly off to Sychar and had a wonderful story to tell to the people there. She is all ablaze with enthusiasm now and is not ashamed of her new faith in the Messiah. These people all knew her sinful life and she has nothing to conceal from them. So she says: "Come see a man who told me all that I have done. Is this the Messiah?" She had done so many wicked things that this fact added piquancy to her story. And she showed a woman's wit in the form of her question. She used the Greek negative (*me*) that threw doubt on the query and really expected the answer, "no." But she was psychologist enough to know that this was the way to excite the curiosity of the people of Sychar instead of starting a debate. She had not expressed a positive conviction. It was a case of too good to be true. So the people streamed out of town, were coming to Jesus in a long line. This was the first Samaritan convert and she became an evangelist of grace on the spot.

Many of the Samaritans from Sychar who came at the woman's invitation believed on Jesus as the Messiah "because of the saying of the woman bearing witness." She did not have much that she could say beyond telling her personal experience that brought the crowd to Jesus.

But these new converts begged Jesus to come

with them to Sychar and preach to them. So he did and remained there two days. It was a short meeting, but a powerful one. "Many more believed because of his preaching and said to the woman: 'No longer are we believing just because of your talk; for we ourselves have heard him, and we know that he is truly the Saviour of the world.'" Jew as he was, they took him as their Messiah and Savior. They had the breadth of vision to see that Jesus was the Savior of the whole world. It is a remarkable outcome. This great Samaritan revival came about in the most incidental way. The woman who was the agent in spreading the glad news of her own conversion was the most unlikely prospect in the town. But, once she was converted to faith in Christ, she wished to share her joy with others, her friends and neighbors. She had courage and skill to take right hold all by herself and to bring the people to Jesus that they might see for themselves. It is pitiful what flimsy excuses we make for our neglect and indifference. It we really took hold right where we are, we could get people to church and to Christ.

It was a joyful time for Jesus. He was leaving Judea for the present because of the jealousy of the rabbis there. He was on his way to Galilee to get away from the opposition of the Pharisees, which was to follow him there. But here in Samaria the soul of Jesus rejoiced at the prospect of the harvest of the world. The conversion of this one Samaritan woman was a prophecy of what could come and what did come so soon at Sychar.

Jesus had no appetite for food brought by the disciples who little understood the ecstasy of Jesus who was feeding on doing the will of his Father who had sent him to do this work. They will know ere long the joy of such work, but now they do not understand the joy of Jesus. We can make Christ happy by personal evangelism. We can bring our friends to Jesus. We can start a revival in our own hearts, our own home, our own church, our own town.

CHAPTER X

Simon Magus the Mercenary Pretender

THE recurrence of pious pretenders during the centuries gives poignancy and pertinency to the story of Simon Magus in Acts 8:9, 24. The very grotesqueness of this bizarre character led some scholars to doubt the historical reality of the picture in Acts. Legend has been busy with the name of this magician. In the so-called Clementine literature of the third century (the *Homilies* in Greek, the *Recognitions* in Latin) Peter is glorified and Paul is denounced. Paul is pictured under the name of Simon who holds debates with Peter in Cæsarea, Tyre, Laodicea, and Antioch. Later legend has Simon denounced by Peter in Rome. It is one of the curiosities of New Testament criticism that Baur made this legend the basis of his theory of *Tendenz* Literature in the New Testament. He denied that Simon Magus was a real character. He was merely a representation of Paul as a term of reproach in his conflict with Peter. So then Baur made Acts a book of compromise to smooth out the rivalry between Peter and Paul and without real historical value. But the Tübingen view of the New Testament has fallen by the way. It is now distinctly a back number.

It is probable that Justin Martyr, himself a native of Samaria, who wrote his *Apology* about a hundred years after the events in Acts 8, identifies Simon Magus with Simon of Gitta, six miles from Sebaste. This identification is by no means certain. The name is common enough and both are real persons. It is probable that Simon of Gitta was nearer to the time of Justin than Simon Magus of Sebaste. We know now that Justin Martyr confused a statue in Rome to the worship of *Semoni Sanco Deo Fidio,* a Sabine god, with the worship of Simon of Gitta, whom he also took to be Simon Magus, whom the Samaritans almost worshiped. Justin called him the first heresiarch, the first founder of heresy. There was a Simonian sect in Justin's day with a large following. Dante (*Inferno,* Canto XIX) cries: "Woe to thee, Simon Magus! Woe to you, his wretched followers!" There is no likelihood that Simon Magus was a full-fledged Gnostic as Justin knew the Gnostics in the second century. But he clearly held to the germs of the later Gnostic doctrines in his talk of "Power" and "Thought" much as modern theosophists do to-day. It is one incidental argument for the early date of Acts that Luke does not picture Simon in terms of the later Gnostics. He came to be regarded as the father of heresy. He was, in truth, the prototype of the later departures from the true faith. In him we see Christianity for the first time at grips with superstition and religious fraud. Such impostors were common-enough in that time. One has only to think of the Emperor

Tiberius on the Island of Capri with his flock of
Chaldaean soothsayers around him to see the prev-
alence of such impostors. In the Acts Luke carries
on the picture in the collision between Paul and
Elymas Barjesus in Cyprus, Paul and the Sons
of Sceva in Ephesus. The twentieth century cannot fling too many stones at the first when we recall the great vogue enjoyed by religious charlatans
to-day in all lands.

The description of Simon Magus in the Acts
gives us all our real information of this mercenary
pretender, this pious fraud, but it is enough. He
had a powerful hold in Samaria (Sebaste) and
had practiced his magical arts that astonished the
people of Samaria. They watched him ("fastened
their minds on him") because for a long time
they were astonished by his tricks. They looked
on him as a god because they could not explain
his deeds. With wide-eyed wonder the old and the
young people, in high places and in lowly homes,
gathered around him as a veritable hero. The recent death of the most famous modern wizard
ought to throw a light on this whole subject, for
he boasted that he could reproduce any tricks of
spiritualistic mediums and no one was able to solve
his gifts. But he died with his secrets unrevealed.

About A. D. 35 a false prophet gave it out that
he could find on Mt. Gerizim the sacred vessels
left there by Moses (though Moses was never
there). Such crowds followed this pretender that
Pontius Pilate sent soldiers to scatter them. It
was done with such slaughter that Pilate was sent

to Rome for trial and was banished to Switzerland.

Simon Magus reveled in the reputation that he
had won in Samaria. He diligently gave it out that
"he himself was some great one." He was by his
own admission a personality of supreme importance. It is positively amazing how gullible people can be. Those who were under his spell kept
saying: "This man is the Power of God that is
called Great." So far from denying it, he rather
implied by hints and chicanery that he was an
emanation from God or *æon* as the Gnostics held,
a common oriental doctrine. The Samaritans were
grossly superstitious while Simon Magus was unprincipled. A form of conceit may have at times
inclined him to belief in his own powers as divine.
But whatever self-delusion he had, he was a conscious impostor. When Philip appeared with his
message that Jesus was the Messiah of Jewish
hope, Simon Magus was naturally interested in
this preaching which presented Jesus as a rival
to himself. Probably at first he scouted it all in
his own mind and took the miracles wrought by
Philip as humbugs like his tricks which fooled
the people. But finally it was clear to him that
Philip had a power that he did not possess. He was
in grave peril of being supplanted by the new doctrine. Apparently there was something in this new
system. So Simon decided to get in on the ground
floor of the thing and find out for himself what
there was in it. So he "believed" as many at the
first passover of Christ's ministry "believed in his
name" (John 2:23), though Jesus "did not believe

in them." So again at the feast of tabernacles "many believed on him" (John 8:30), while Jesus uncovered their shallow and unreliable belief. In the case of Simon Magus he may have accepted Jesus as an equal or even superior to himself, but he did not take him as Savior from sin and Lord of his life. He submitted to baptism also, though he had not undergone the spiritual change symbolized by the ordinance. He may have regarded baptism as a sort of magical charm or spell that might initiate him into whatever mysteries Christianity might have. So the Mithraists had a bloodbath (*taurobolium*) which was supposed to work a magical change at initiation.

There is an Old Testament parallel to Simon Magus to be found in Gehazi who made money out of the baptism of Naaman in the Jordan (2 Kings V). It is significant how closely Simon "clung to Philip and beholding signs and great miracles taking place kept on being astonished." The Greek word means literally "stood out of himself." He almost jumped out of his skin with jealousy when he saw the reality of the work of Philip. Simon was now in this Samaritan church, but he had not discovered the secret of Philip's power.

The coming of Peter and John to Samaria to investigate the work of Philip among the Samaritans brought a new crisis to Simon Magus. They wholly endorsed what had been done in Samaria. One can recall that John (and James) had even wanted to call down fire on the Samaritans for their cold reception of Christ and his workers. But

John has learned much since then. These Samaritan Christians were not baptized again. They had already believed and were baptized, but they had not received the special gift of the Holy Spirit such as came at the great Pentecost in Jerusalem. So Peter and John prayed for the Samaritan believers that they might receive this special gift. Later such a gift came on Cornelius and his company before their baptism and also still later on some ill-informed disciples of John the Baptist who were converted and baptized and then spoke with tongues and prophesied. Evidently the Samaritan Christians spoke with tongues also for Simon Magus "saw that by the laying on of the hands of the Apostles the Holy Spirit was bestowed on them." Here at last he seemed to be getting close to what he wanted. He simply must get this new "power" that he might retain or regain his influence with the people.

He acted on the principle of the devil that every man has his price. He knew that he did himself. He came up to Peter and John and "offered them money," probably holding the coins in his palm as he said: "Give to me also this power that on whomsoever I lay my hands he may keep on receiving the Holy Spirit." It was a dastardly proposition that stirred Peter to the depths of his soul with indignation. He had seen Peter transfer power to others. This human agency appears in Acts 2:4, 33; 4:31; 10:44, but Simon thought he only had to buy it to pass it on. If he could only get this power from Peter, then there was no limit to his power and influence. He simply took Peter and John to be more accomplished sorcerers than he was, who could be induced by bribing to tell their secret to him and share their power with him.

These two Simons, Simon Peter and Simon Magus, confronted each other. Peter had his own weaknesses and cowardice had been one of them in the hour of his own denials. But he is now a rock in reality and the temptation found no lodgment in his soul. With noble majesty he replied: "Thy money perish with thee, because thou actually didst suppose that thou couldst obtain the gift of God with money." Simon is not the only one who has had the audacity to try this scheme for selfish ecclesiastical promotion, but his very name has been given to this sin and crime. "Simony" it is called to-day in England when one seeks to obtain office in the Church of England by the use of money. This treatment of sacred functions as a marketable thing is contemptible and others besides clergymen are guilty of it. One of the losses from the union of church and state is precisely this thing, but many people look to money as the means of securing spiritual privileges and prerogatives. There is surely need to-day for alertness on the part of all that they do not fall into this only too common sin. The poorest can get as close to God as the richest. An example of "Simony" occurred as early as the third century and many councils condemned it.

But Peter had still more to say to Simon Magus:

"There is no part nor lot to thee in this matter, for thy heart is not straight before God." He had said that he "believed" and had been baptized, but it was all false, "for I see that you are in the gall of bitterness and the bond of iniquity" (cf. Psalm 78:37). He had forsaken the straight way and had followed the way of Balaam, who loved the hire of wrong-doing (2 Pet. 2:15.). It was a sad outcome, but Peter had the courage to tear off the mask from this wolf in sheep's clothing and to reveal him in his true character.

Peter urges repentance and prayer: "Repent therefore of this thy wickedness if perchance the thought of thy heart will be forgiven thee." Peter clearly thinks that Simon Magus has come near to the unpardonable sin of blasphemy against the Holy Spirit. It was clear that he had never really repented or been converted. He was a charlatan and a shark, an impostor who wanted to traffic in spiritual things to his own advantage.

Simon Magus was taken aback at this sudden and unsparing exposure of his real self by Simon Peter. He said in reply: "Pray to the Lord for me that no one of these things of which you have spoken come upon me." He did not wish to pay the penalty for his great sin. Most criminals feel that way. But there is no evidence whatever that he ever repented and turned to the Lord. The root of the matter was not in him. He slunk back into his own hollow chicanery and went on trying to deceive the people. It is a tragedy that the Christian ministry is sometimes used by pretenders as a cloak to fleece the lambs. Jesus warned men against these wolves in sheep's clothing. Some of them, said Jesus, will almost deceive the very elect.

CHAPTER XI

HEROD ANTIPAS AND HERODIAS HOME WRECKERS

THE Gospels and Josephus give a vivid picture of two despicable characters in high life who serve as a warning to loose livers to-day. They are Herod Antipas and Herodias who represent the very worst elements of the time and yet who lived in the lime-light of political and social leadership.

Herod Antipas was the second son of Herod the Great and Malthace of Samaria, one of his ten wives. She was thus a Samaritan woman and only half-Jew at the most, while Herod the Great was an Idumæan. Josephus calls this Idumæan-Samaritan (only one-quarter Jew) Herod (*Antiquities*, XVIII. ii. 1) or Antipas (*Antiquities*, XVII. vii. 1). In the New Testament and in the coins he is simply termed "Herod." In the second of his father's wills he had been designated his sole successor, with the title of king, but in the last will he was to receive only Galilee and Perea with the title of tetrarch. In Mark 6:14f, and Matthew 14:9 he is called king in popular parlance. He contested this last will of Herod the Great, but Augustus sustained the will and Archelaus was given his chance in Judea (Josephus, *Antiquities*, XVII. xi. 4). Herod Antipas ruled as tetrarch from B. C.

4 to A. D. 39. When Joseph heard in Egypt that Archelaus was to get Judea, he was afraid to go to Bethlehem to live and so went back to Nazareth where Jesus spent his youth (Matthew 2:22–3).

Most of the active ministry of Jesus was spent in Galilee or Perea under the rule of this man who did not see him till the end. He was a builder of cities like his father and made Tiberias his capital, which still exists. Decapolis, a Greek region of ten cities, came in between Galilee and Perea and yet Herod Antipas managed to govern both sections with some skill. He had been educated at Rome with Archelaus and Philip and was not a man of integrity of character. Jesus warned his disciples against "the leaven of Herod" (Mark 8:15), probably his political trickery. He likewise called him "that fox" (Luke 13:31) when the Pharisees showed unusual interest in Jesus then in Perea. He informed them that he was in no sense afraid of the time-server, "for it cannot be that a prophet perish out of Jerusalem."

His brother Herod Philip, son of Herod the Great, and Mariamne (daughter of Simon of Jerusalem, the high priest), lived in Rome with his wife Herodias, daughter of Aristobulus (son of Mariamne, granddaughter of Hyrcanus II) and so a Maccabee, and niece of her own husband. On one occasion when in Rome at his brother Philip's house Antipas seduced Herodias and persuaded her to leave her husband and to come to him. It was a case of infatuation on both sides, like the affinity excuses in modern life and novels. She agreed to leave Philip, though they had a daughter, Salome, on condition that Antipas get rid of his own wife, a daughter of Aretas, king of the Nabataeans. When she heard that her husband, Antipas, had actually agreed to this dastardly proposal, she fled for refuge to her father, King Aretas, who waged war against him, A. D. 36, apparently nine years after her flight from Antipas. The severe defeat of Antipas by Aretas was interpreted by some to be a punishment by God for what he had done to John the Baptist (Josephus, *Antiquities,* XVIII. v. 2) as well as for his treatment of the daughter of Aretas. Vitellius, the Roman general, was under orders to go to the help of Antipas. The Romans did not like the pretensions of Aretas. But Vitellius had gone no further than Jerusalem when he heard of the death of the Emperor Tiberius (A. D. 37).

After the departure of his wife to her father, Aretas, somewhere about A. D. 25, Antipas married Herodias who had left her husband, Herod Philip, in Rome. It was as sorry a mess as anything that besmirches marriage to-day. Each divorced the husband or wife in order to marry. Antipas and Herodias were close kin, uncle and niece, an atrocious thing in itself from the Jewish standpoint. Women did sometimes divorce their husbands then as Salome, sister of Herod the Great, had done, and now as Herodias had done. But it was adultery in each case, as Mark 10:11 and 12 reports Jesus as saying, and in Matthew 5:32 and 19:9, remarriage of the innocent party is alone allowed. This flagrant conduct on the part of Herod Antipas and Herodias outraged the best Jewish public sentiment (Lev. 18:16; 20:21).

During the ministry of John the Baptist there was still indignant talk about it. It is possible that John was inveigled into Perea and into talk about this infamous marriage by the Pharisees who disliked him and who keenly resented his comparing them to broods of vipers (Matt. 3:7). They could easily draw him out by questions to take a stand on this marriage. But, however the issue was raised, John did not hesitate to condemn it in unmeasured terms, reproving Antipas "for Herodias his brother's wife and for all the evil things which Herod had done" (Luke 3:19). It seems that John was actually brought into the presence of Herod Antipas and Herodias, "for John said unto Herod: 'It is not lawful for thee to have thy brother's wife'" (Mark 6:18). At any rate "Herod himself had sent forth and laid hold upon John, and bound him in prison for the sake of Herodias, his brother Philip's wife; for he had married her" (Mark 6:17). This prison was at Machaerus, a powerful fortress, east of the Dead Sea (Josephus, *War,* VII. vi). It is plain in the Gospels that both Antipas and Herodias had a private grudge against John for his plain words to them. It is refreshing to find a preacher of righteousness who is not afraid to expose immorality in high places at the risk of his own life. Josephus says that Herod "feared lest the great influence that John had over the people might put it into his power and inclination to raise a rebellion" (*Antiquities*, XVIII. v. 2). But this is merely the public and political reason given by Josephus and in no way conflicts with the private anger cherished by him toward the brave prophet. Herod Antipas put John in prison and kept him in prison.

The real feeling of Herod toward John is a bit difficult to understand. Matthew 14:5 says that he wanted to put him to death, but feared the multitude who counted him as a prophet. But Mark (6:20) says that "Herod feared John, knowing that he was a righteous man and a holy, and kept him safe. And when he heard him, he was much perplexed and he heard him gladly." By combining the two statements we see that Herod really knew that John was right and was deeply impressed by his discourses in the prison. He had, however, spells of indignation against him for his plain and bold denunciation of Herodias and himself, which he apparently kept up, though a prisoner. These moods of rage were largely due to the constant prodding of Herodias, who "set herself against him (literally, had it in for him); and desired to kill him, and she could not." Herodias was a desperate woman and was determined to get vengeance on this preacher who had denounced her.

Herod had an uneasy conscience, it is plain, but Herodias watched her chance which came on the birthday of Herod when he made a supper to his lords and leaders at Machaerus. Herodias let her daughter Salome come in to dance before these dignitaries, a regular oriental licentious dance, in order to get power over Antipas when he became tipsy from the wine. So pleased was Antipas with the girl's exhibition of herself, that he gave his oath to give her what she wished, even to half of his kingdom. Probably Herodias expected this result and she was ready when Salome came out and said to her: "What shall I ask?" The answer was at hand, "The head of John the Baptist." "The king was exceeding sorry, but for the sake of his oaths, and of them that sat at meat, he would not reject her" (Mark 6:26). So the head of John the Baptist was brought into the feast to Herodias on a charger. The inference of the grewsome story (Mark 6:19–29; Matt. 14:6–12) is that Herodias gloated over her victim and Salome exulted in her sensual triumph, while Antipas in his muddled mind from drink and debauchery, sought to justify his brutality by respect for his oath in the presence of his guests. This was no road-house or bagnio, but the palace and fortress of the ruler of Galilee and Perea when his birthday feast was in progress. Wine, lewd dancing, murder. It is a modern combination and as old as human history. Herodias had sunk so low that she flung her own daughter into this drunken crowd to carry out her will against John the Baptist. The only noble picture here is that of John, who lost his head for his courage, but who towers still above them all. One thinks of Elijah before Ahab and Jezebel. Herodias was as relentless as Jezebel, but John did not run away, could not in fact.

It is plain that Herod Antipas was deeply grieved

over this outcome when he recovered from his
drunken spree. The third tour of Galilee by Jesus,
when he sent the Apostles out by twos, created a
tremendous sensation. Herod had never seen Jesus,
but he had seen John and still saw him at night as
the head on a charger came slipping towards him
in the dark. So he said unto his servants about
Jesus: "This is John the Baptist; he is risen from
the dead; and therefore do these powers work in
him" (Matt. 14:2). He asked the people what they
made of it all and the answers perplexed him still
more (Luke 9:7). Some said it was Elijah, others
agreed with Herod that it was John the Baptist
come to life. But Herod argued: "John I be' eaded;
but who is this about whom I hear such things?"
(Luke 9:9). If he could only see him, but Jesus
kept out of the way of this sly old "fox" who had
had John beheaded. When he did see Jesus at his
trial, Jesus kept absolute silence and wrought no
miracles for his curiosity. Pilate had made friends
by this courtesy, but he still had Jesus on his hands.

Both Herod Antipas and Herodias disappear
from the New Testament story. Josephus (*Antiquities*, XVIII. vii. 2) gives the sad sequel which
shows how powerful was the hold of Herodias on
Antipas. When the young scapegrace, Herod
Agrippa II, boon companion of Caius Caligula, the
Emperor, won a crown, it was too much for Herodias. He had once been a mere beggar and unable
to pay his spendthrift debts. So Herodias prodded
Herod Antipas against his judgment to go to Rome
and to beg of Caligula the title of King instead of

Tetrarch. But young Agrippa took advantage of this opportunity to reveal to Caligula the military supplies collected by Herod Antipas as if against Caligula. The result was that Antipas lost A. D. 39 the tetrarchy of Galilee and Perea, which went to young Agrippa while Antipas was sent in banishment to Lyons in Gaul. Caligula excused Herodias, who was really the cause of it all, but she accompanied her husband and proudly took her medicine with what grace she could. One wastes no sympathy upon the fate of this couple of home-wreckers. The lurid light of their wicked lives flares up beside the steady flame of John the Baptist and of Jesus our Lord.

CHAPTER XII

THE OPEN-EYED CHAMPION OF JESUS

ONE wishes that one knew the name of the fine spirit so brilliantly sketched in John 9:1-38. For some reason the Fourth Gospel does not give his name. But it is quite worth while to study him carefully even if we do not know his name. It is difficult to think that he is a legendary character as some modern scholars think. It is far simpler to accept the historicity of the narrative than to believe in the creative genius of the author. The whole story hangs together with wonderful verisimilitude and has pith and point for us to-day when some are timid about the claims of Jesus to deity.

The narrative opens with the puzzle of the disciples over the theological problem of the responsibility for the blindness of the unfortunate man (John 9:1-5), whether, since he was born blind, the sin was that of his parents or of the man himself. There is such a thing as disease caused by the sin of one's parents, a lamentable fact. How to prevent the birth of children by mental defectives and by hopelessly diseased parents is a real problem to-day. Some of the states in America have rigid laws on the subject. In the case of the lame man he had brought disease on himself by his own sin

(John 5:14). But the result (consecutive use of *hina* in 9:2) in the case of the man born blind was not his fault or that of his parents. Jesus affirms that God had a purpose in the man's tragedy. There is a comfort in this thought for many of us with our many limitations. God can and often does over-rule them for his glory and for working his own will. The phrase "the works of God" leads Jesus to link us with himself. The correct text in 9:4 is "We must work the works of him who sent me." There is dignity in this high association with Jesus in the works of God. There is power in it also. Linked with Christ, the Light of the world, we can shed light on others and use the power of God in Christ. So Jesus gave the disciples a profound philosophy of Christian work that should cheer all to-day who are pushing on the program of Christ for the redemption of the world.

The discussion over, Jesus voluntarily proceeded to heal the blind man who apparently had not asked or expected healing. Jesus was passing along and saw the man sitting at his usual place and begging alms as he had been doing all his life. The disciples had called the attention of Jesus to the man and much of good came out of their theological specula-tion, though they themselves apparently had no hope that Jesus would cure the man born blind (9:32). One cannot believe that Jesus made use of the clay and the spittle because there was any value in it, though some of the ancients did attach heal-ing virtue to the spittle. The power to heal rested in Jesus Christ who only occasionally used any intermediate agencies. Sometimes he employed the touch, but often it was a mere word. The use of spittle and clay would make the man willing to obey Jesus and go to the Pool of Siloam. But why was he sent to the water at all? Perhaps this act of obedience had some influence on the man's attitude. It was objective and may have counted for something in the man's own psychology. Coöperating with nature and helping the powers of nature often restores health. But here nature was completely defeated by this case of blindness. It was a simple thing that Jesus commanded. "He went off therefore and washed himself and came seeing." The impossible had happened and he was seeing the wonderful world for the first time. He did not know the name of the wonderful man who had healed him, but he knew that his eyes were opened however ignorant he might be of the method employed. Many patients to-day bear like witness to the skill and prowess of physicians and surgeons who have saved their lives.

The man had been a beggar all his life and so went back to his trade, but with wide open eyes (9:8–12). He had his regular stand and was apparently well known to those who passed him there. They had never seen him with his eyes open before. However, some men are fakirs and pose as blind men with blind days, so that a dispute arose among them concerning his identity. Some asked: "Is not this the fellow who used to sit and beg?" Others were positive and said: "This is he." Still others regarded it as a case of similarity or mistaken identity. "Not a bit of it, but he is just like him." So the matter stood till the man could bear it no longer. He had to speak: "I am the man." But this solution only increased their curiosity: "How then were your eyes opened?" It was a natural question, if he was not a fraud. He did not himself know how the thing had been done. He could only tell the bare facts which he did. He only knew him as "the man called Jesus." But the inquirers were not satisfied: "Where is he?" They wanted to question Jesus about it. But the man could only say: "I do not know."

So they appealed to the Pharisees as responsible theological guides who ought to be able to solve all difficulties (9:13–16). This is the chief use that some people have for preachers and teachers. It is to settle theological disputes and untie hard knots. The Pharisees looked wise and solemn in their inquiry and brought out the fact that the thing was done by Jesus on the Sabbath day. But this item at once divided these doctors of the law. Some bluntly concluded: "This man (Jesus) is not from God, because he does not keep the Sabbath" (their ideas of the Sabbath as had been expressed before, John 5:18). But others of the Pharisees went further and asked: "How is a sinful man able to do such things?" It was a hard nut to crack. No wonder that a schism arose among the Pharisees on the point. They were not able to throw any light on the problem.

The Pharisees then turn to the man himself for help in their dilemma (9:17): "What do you say about him, since he opened your eyes?" It was a helpless and pitiful appeal by the theologians. All that he could say was: "He is a prophet." He did not really know any more.

The hostile Jews turn to the man's parents to see if there was not some slip in the thing somewhere, because they did not really believe that the man actually was born blind (9:18–23). This appeal was also a confession of failure on the part of the Jewish leaders. They were trying to save their faces, as pastmasters of wisdom. They really ask three questions in one: "Is this your son, who you say was born blind? How then does he now see?" It was adroit, but the parents knew more about Jesus than their son and also more of the animosity of the Jews whom they feared, because they had already plotted to turn out of the synagogue those who confessed Jesus as Messiah. They did not wish to run that risk. So the parents answered that he is their son and was born blind. They could certify to that, but they declined to say who had opened his eyes and how and passed that problem over to the son: "Ask him, he is of age, he will speak for himself." It was a skillful turn that completely discomfited the rabbis.

Once again they turn to the once-blind man, their only alternative in their theological tangle over the facts (9:24–34). To admit the facts would be to admit the claims of Jesus as Messiah. This time they take the turn of proposing that, if the fact is admitted, Jesus gets no credit for it: "Give glory to God. We know this man is a sinner." This was a distinct retreat from the position that a sinner could not do such a deed and, if it was done, it proved that Jesus was from God (9:16). They had to do something and they stand upon the other foot and claim their theological omniscience in spite of their proved incompetence. By this time the once-blind man's sense of humor is aroused. He knows little about Jesus save what he did to him, but he uses raillery and sarcasm as he lays bare the hopeless inconsistencies of these wiseacres. The man was quick in his pungent repartee: "Whether he is a sinner I do not know; one thing I do know, that though once blind, I now see." It was a homethrust and brushed aside all the pettifogging subterfuges of the Pharisees. They weakly ask again: "What did he do to you? How did he open your eyes?" The man's answer cut to the very quick: "I told you already and you did not listen. Why do you want to hear it again? Do you also wish to become his disciples?" This dig was too much, so that they reviled him with being the disciple of Jesus, which was not yet true. Sermons and hymns have misinterpreted the man's words about the opening of his eyes. The Pharisees claimed to be the disciples of Moses to whom God had spoken: "But this fellow we do not know whence he is." The man quickly saw the opening and waded right in: "Why herein is the wonder that you do not know whence he is and yet he opened my eyes." There is no answer to this sarcasm. He reminds them of their dictum that God does not hear sinners and yet he had opened his eyes: "If this man were not from God, he could

not do anything." He turned their own words to
their own confusion. The end comes to a tension
like this with withering scorn from the Pharisees:
"You were begotten, all of you, in sins and yet you
are trying to teach us." The ignorant upstart was
actually rebuking the learned professional ex-
pounders of the law! It was the limit and was not
to be endured. So they cast him out of the synagogue for his uppishness in getting the best of the
rabbis and exposing their theological quibbles before the public. The ounce of fact in this man's experience had put to rout a whole windbag of
reactionary and traditional theologizing.

The sequel is most interesting (9:35–40). Jesus
heard what the Pharisees had done to the man for
his valiant opposition to them. So he hunted him
up and said to him: "Do you believe on the Son
of man?" That was a piece of theology beyond his
knowledge. Se he merely says: "And who is he, sir,
that I may believe on him?" Jesus pointedly says:
"You have both seen him and he is the one who is
talking with you." The moment of decision for the
man had come. He was ready by the experience
that he had had. He surrendered on the spot: "I
believe, Lord." He would believe any claim made
by Jesus. So he worshiped him as Messiah and
Savior. God uses all his dealings with us to focus
them all on the great moment of crisis. Jesus had
won the open-eyed champion, this outcast from the
synagogue, this able and alert contender of the now
new faith. Jesus had lost the Pharisees who posed
as guides and lights. Their spiritual eyes were more

blind than ever, though they could still see with their physical eyes. But this once-blind man had his eyes open to see the wondrous world and the eyes of his heart were now open to see the glory of Jesus. It mattered little now what the Pharisees thought about him or did to him. He had seen the light of the knowledge of the glory of God in the face of Jesus Christ.

CHAPTER XIII

GAMALIEL THE THEOLOGICAL OPPORTUNIST

SCHOLARS are unable to agree on the spirit and motives of Gamaliel I in his championship of Peter and the other apostles who were brought again before the Sanhedrin for disobedience and for the charge that they were responsible for the blood of Jesus (Acts 5:28). Peter boldly affirmed that they must obey God rather than man (5:29) and repeated his charge and reaffirmed the fact of the resurrection of Jesus of which he and the other apostles were witnesses. The Sanhedrin were cut to the heart as if a saw had sawn them in two and wanted to kill them on the spot though they no longer had the power to put to death. They could only do so illegally by mob law as they later did in the case of Stephen. It was a real crisis that confronted the Sanhedrin, composed, as it was, of both Pharisees and Sadducees, though the President of the Sanhedrin until after the destruction of Jerusalem was a Sadducee (the chief priest) and not a Pharisaic rabbi. After the destruction of the temple the Sadducees and priests lost their influence. Whatever was done had to be done quickly, if Peter and the apostles were not to be stoned as Stephen was later. The attacks made against Peter,

John and the rest had so far been made by the Sadducees on the ground that they proclaimed in Jesus the resurrection from the dead (Acts 4:2–5: 17). Meanwhile the Pharisees were apparently quiescent until Stephen stirred them into hostility. Then the Sadducees were bent on a policy of destruction. What were the Pharisees to do at this crisis? It is at this juncture that Gamaliel steps forth as their spokesman.

Gamaliel (Reward of God) was the grandson of Hillel, the rival of Shammai and founder of the more liberal of the two theological schools of the Pharisees in Jerusalem. Furneaux (*The Acts,* p. 79) suggests that "Gamaliel may have been one of the doctors in the midst of whom the boy Jesus had sat, hearing and asking questions (Lu. 2:47)." At any rate we know that he had great influence in the Sanhedrin as the leader of the Pharisaic party. He was the first of the seven Jewish doctors of the law to be called *Rabban* like *Rabboni* applied to Jesus by Mary Magdelene (John 20:16). Once when Gamaliel was absent from the Sanhedrin, their decision to appoint a leap-year was to be valid only if Gamaliel agreed (Mishna, *Edajoth* vii:7). He had a grandson named Gamaliel II while he was himself later termed Gamaliel the Elder (*ha-zākēn*). He was a man of scholarly tastes as shown by his studies in Greek literature and by his advice to his students to follow his example in the study of Greek writers. The narrower rabbis thought that the study of Greek literature was as bad as Egyptian thaumaturgy. His more liberal outlook on life is shown by his teaching that the Jews should greet the heathen with "Peace be with you" even on a heathen feast day. He also taught that poor Gentiles should have the same right to glean the harvest fields as poor Jews. So also he championed the cause of wives against unprincipled husbands and of widows against greedy children. In fact the Mishna says (*Sota* ix:15) that "with the death of Gamaliel the reverence for the law ceased and purity and abstinence died away." It is plain also that Paul was proud of the fact that he had sat at the feet of Galamiel while a student in Jerusalem (Acts 22:3). It is a great experience for a brilliant student to have a great personality for a teacher. One thinks of Aristotle as the teacher of Alexander the Great. It is small wonder that young Saul cut forward in Judaism beyond his fellow students (Gal. 1:14.). It is plain that Gamaliel was the outstanding Pharisee of his day in the Sanhedrin as he was later considered the glory of the law. Annas and Caiaphas and John and Alexander were the leaders of the Sadducees in the attacks upon the Apostles (Acts 4:5 and 6). Against Jesus at first the Pharisees took the lead and only later the Sadducees joined them. Now the Sadducees were the aggressors while the Pharisees were reluctant to line up with the Sadducees where the doctrine of the resurrection was the issue.

But now Gamaliel came to the fore. What was his real attitude in this crisis, this "doctor of the law held in honor by all the people?" He first desired that the apostles be put out for a brief space that the Sanhedrin might discuss the problem without the embarrassment of their presence. Precisely this precaution had been taken once before (Acts 4:15). Then Gamaliel proceeded to give his interpretation of the situation in the nature of a *caveat* to the Sadducees who were bent on blood: "Ye men of Israel, take heed to yourselves in the case of these men as to what you are about to do." The members of the Sanhedrin were on trial, as well as the apostles. In this warning Gamaliel was undoubtedly right. That is always true in every emergency. But Gamaliel does not pointedly say that the apostles were innocent of any wrongdoing and should therefore be set free. He rather appeals to the self-interest of the Sadducees who might be running greater risks than they understood. In proof of his warning Gamaliel cites two historical examples of men who made great pretensions and who had come to naught by the natural course of events. The first is that of Theudas. Now Josephus (*Antiquities* xx. 5:1) tells of Theudas, a false prophet, who won a large following. He promised to divide the river Jordan as Joshua had done. But Cuspius Fadus, the Roman Procurator, sent a squadron of horse who slew many and took prisoners also and scattered the rest. Theudas himself was beheaded. So the episode came to naught. But this incident in Josephus occurred A. D. 46, ten years or more after the speech of Gamaliel. The event in Luke would have to be thirty years before that in Josephus. Hence a chronological historical difficulty arises with various solutions that are

offered. The easiest one is to say that either Luke
or Josephus has made a blunder in the date. The
blame used to be placed on Luke on the ground that
Josephus is more reliable as a historian. But Luke's
credibility has received strong reënforcement by
the new discoveries in the papyri and the inscrip-
tions, and Josephus has many errors in his writings. Another solution is that both are correct and
refer to different men. Josephus tells of four men
named Simon within forty years and three named
Judas within ten years who were instigators of rebellion. This can be said to those who consider it
improbable that two men of the same name within
thirty years should make false claims and meet a
like fate. Besides, the name Theudas is abbreviated
and may come from Theodosius, Theodorus, Theo-
dotus, etc. As matters stand now one will credit
Luke or Josephus according to his prejudices and
predilections. There is no trouble about the case of
Judas the Galilean (also Gaulonite) except that
the first failures of Judas the Galilean suits the
early date for Gamaliel's speech. Later the cause
of Judas the Galilean rallied again and made still
more trouble. So thus the two instances given by
Gamaliel are pertinent to his point. Theudas gave
himself out as a man of importance ("somebody")
and gathered four hundred followers, but he was
slain and his party dissolved and came to nothing.
Judas the Galilean in this early stage belonged to
the time of the enrollment (census), the second
one under Augustus, A. D. 6. This puts the date of
Theudas in Luke still earlier, for Luke says that

Judas came "after this one" (Theudas). Judas himself perished and his followers were scattered, even though in later years some of them did rally again. So much for the historical illustrations.

Now for the application, "now as to the present situation," Gamaliel draws his own conclusion along the line of his advice: "Stand off from and leave them alone." The Bezan text adds "and defile not your hands." But Gamaliel argues the case further: "Because if this counsel or this work be from men (a condition of the third class with the subjunctive mode, undetermined, but with probability of being determined), it will be overthrown; but if it is from God (a first-class condition with the indicative, assuming it to be true), you will not be able to overthrow them (the Bezan text adds, 'Neither ye nor kings nor despots. Refrain therefore from these men'), lest perchance ye be found even fighting against God." It was a powerful message, shrewd and convincing, that carried conviction for the moment. The Pharisees were in the majority in the Sanhedrin and they yielded assent to his doctrine of letting things go for the present. So the apostles were called in and beaten for having disobeyed the previous command to stop preaching Jesus and were told again not to speak in the name of Jesus and were set free.

But what were the real motives of Gamaliel in scoring this victory over the Sadducees for such it was? Some men even say that Gamaliel had become a convert to Christianity, but was afraid to show his colors even now, a secret disciple like

Nicodemus and Joseph of Arimathea, who had like them been really opposed to the crucifixion of Christ. But there is no real evidence for this interpretation. And the Talmud affirms that Gamaliel died a Jew. Some, like Wendt, deny that Gamaliel made this speech and consider it the invention of Luke, just as Baur holds that the peace-loving Gamaliel could not have been the teacher of the fanatical young Saul who came to relish the slaughter of the saints. One needs common sense in the interpretation of history and the avoidance of fanciful and whimsical difficulties. It is common enough for pupils to go beyond the master in extremes. It is to be noted also that, in the case of Stephen, Gamaliel did not lift his hand to stop the lynching, for the Pharisees, not the Sadducees, were attacking Stephen.

It is true that Gamaliel used the language of one who knew the power of God as the decisive factor in human affairs. As a broad generalization his point is true that it does not pay to fight against God. As Furneaux well says, immediate success is no criterion of the truth, and in the beginning of things the right often lies with the minority. But in the end God's power is felt. Some present Gamaliel as a teacher of tolerance, a humane, and liberal-minded man. But he may have feared to antagonize the growing power of the Christians in Jerusalem and to have had what Milligan calls "a prudential dread of violent measures." Others still regard Gamaliel as a mere time-server without real convictions and unwilling to take a positive stand against the apostles or against the reactionaries among the Pharisees as well as the Sadducees. Probably that view gives too low a conception of this really able man. But it is difficult not to feel that he really desired a temporizing policy as more likely to succeed against the apostles than violent oppression. So he took the attitude of a cool and wise deliberation and "advocated an opportunist policy" as Rackham holds. The fight before Stephen's day was between the apostles and the Sadducees on the doctrine of the resurrection. His attitude need not be called cynical, but it was that of the ordinary politician (Ewald, Knowling). He had good rabbinical backing also for his interpretation of Providence. Neander holds that Gamaliel was too wise a man to stir a fanatical movement, such as he considered Christianity, into a violent flame. Knowling thinks that the principle of Gamaliel enunciated in his speech shows "his abhorrence of wrangling and over-scrupulosity" and "a proof of his adherence to traditionalism." Like other great rabbis he had his saying that was passed on: "Procure thyself a teacher, avoid being in doubt; and do not accustom thyself to give tithes by guess." The advice is good, but it is that of a thorough Pharisee. On the point of being in doubt he probably would say, as Davy Crockett used to say, that one must be sure that he is right and then go ahead. The path did not seem clear to him about the punishment of the apostles and so he urged caution.

There are times, of course, when the general principle of letting things drift is wise. It is easy enough to take dogmatic positions on doubtful points. That does not help matters at all. On the other hand a policy of undue timidity and fear robs one of courage and power. Gamaliel failed to understand Christianity because of the grip of Pharisaism on his mind and life. He disliked the Sadducees intensely and was glad of the chance to score a point against them. He was a theological opportunist and was unwilling to take a decided stand for the gospel or against it. He was in favor of drifting. In the end he was still a confirmed Pharisee. He did not follow his brilliant pupil Saul whom he probably looked on as his probable successor. What he thought of Saul when he turned to Christ we can only guess.

CHAPTER XIV

Felix the Grafter

Luke gives a fairly clear picture of Felix in Acts 23 and 24. Josephus (*Antiquities,* Book XX, Chapter 8; *War,* Book II, Chapter 13) gives a sketch of Felix that is quite in harmony with that in Acts. He tells of the numerous robber bands that infested Palestine and that gave a vast deal of trouble. Felix slew a great many of them. Josephus may be allowed his customary exaggeration, but a basis of fact must lie behind his statement: "Felix took Eleazar the arch-robber, and many that were with him, alive, when they had ravaged the country for twenty years together, and sent them to Rome; but as to the number of robbers whom he caused to be crucified, and of those who were caught among them, and whom he brought to punishment, they were a multitude not to be enumerated." Felix came to be regarded as a terror to the lawless robber bands, though he was not above using them for his own purposes in order to slay the high priest Jonathan. As a result the robbers grew bolder than ever for they felt sure of the connivance of Felix the Roman Procurator. Josephus moralizes upon the situation thus: "And this seems to me to have been the reason why God, out of his hatred of these men's wickedness, rejected our city; and as for the

temple, he no longer considered it sufficiently pure
for him to inhabit therein, but he brought the
Romans upon us, and threw a fire upon the city to
purge it; and brought upon us, our wives, and
children, slavery, as desirous to make us wiser by
our calamities." It is interesting to place beside
this philosophy of woe the doom of Jerusalem as
foretold by Jesus with the reasons for it. At any
rate the disorders under Felix were not suppressed,
but broke out afresh in a new place.

Felix himself is pictured as more hurtful than
all the robbers. Tacitus is scornful of him as one
"who used the powers of a king with the disposition
of a slave" (*Hist.* V. 9). The state of Palestine
grew constantly worse. At one time thirty thousand
fanatics followed "the Egyptian" mentioned by
Claudius Lysias in Acts 21:38. His cruelty stim-
ulated the Zealots to form fighting bands called
Sicarii (Assassins) who helped bring on the War
with Rome. Felix, according to Tacitus (*Ann.* xii.
54), "deemed that he might perpetrate any ill-deeds
with impunity." It is small wonder that his cruel-
ties ended in disaster. Though a man of low origin
he was allowed both military and civil power
(Suetonius, *Claud.* 28). His final and fatal misstep
was at Cæsarea when in a disturbance between the
Jews and the Syrians he was investigated and "he
had certainly been brought to punishment, unless
Nero had yielded to the importunate solicitations
of his brother Pallas" (Josephus, *Antiquities* XX.
viii. 9). He was recalled as a result of his complic-
ity in the civil war there.

He was a freedman, like his brother Pallas, the rather infamous favorite of Claudius. Tacitus calls him "Antonius Felix." The Latin adjective *felix* is seen in our English "felicitous." He was appointed by Claudius to be Procurator of Judea in succession to Cumanus, probably A. D. 53, though that is not certain. Tacitus says that he had married a granddaughter of Antony and Cleopatra whom he calls Drusilla, probably an error in the name. Suetonius mentions another princess as his wife also. But in the Acts Drusilla is the mistress of Felix. She left her husband, Azisus, the King of Emesa, for this liaison with Felix. Felix is pictured in far darker colors in Josephus, Tacitus, and Suetonius than in Luke, but his chicanery is plain in the Acts. He had a cynical disregard for justice, an open contempt for morality, a frank greed for money quite plain in his conduct towards Paul. These traits are modern enough for any student of present day history.

Claudius Lysias was glad to be rid of the puzzling case of Paul about whom he could learn nothing definite from the mob or the Sanhedrin. His letter to Felix makes the false claim that he had rescued Paul from the mob, "having learned that he was a Roman" (Acts 23:27) in order to cover up the fact that he had been about to scourge a Roman citizen (Acts 22:25). It is worth while to follow the reaction of Felix to Paul.

It began suspiciously enough. When Paul was presented to him, he said: "I will hear thee fully, when thine accusers also are come" (Acts 23:35).

Lysias had directed that these "accusers" make
their accusations against Paul. It took them five
days to come down to Cæsarea and Ananias brought
a Roman lawyer or pleader, "an orator, one Tertullus" (Acts 24:1), who "informed the governor against him" in regular style. It is interesting
to observe the skillful flattery employed by the Roman orator, as he begins his plea against Paul:
"Seeing that by thee we enjoy much peace," a statement belied by all that the historians tell us of the
riots and banditry. Tertullus proceeds: "and that
by thy forethought reforms are coming to this nation," or "evils are being corrected for this nation."
Such unvarnished flattery could only provoke a
smile, but it would sound well to Felix even though
he knew that it was untrue. "We accept it in all
ways and in all places, most excellent Felix, with
all thankfulness." Public officers and politicians in
particular are quite open to fulsome praise. There
are some preachers who are not above listening to
it. Lysias had said that he found against Paul only
"questions of their law, but to have nothing laid to
his charge worthy of death." From the official
standpoint, therefore, Felix could be quite disposed
to give Paul a fair hearing. The charges that Tertullus brought against Paul were that (1) he was a
"pestilent fellow," Paul the pest in a word, (2) "a
mover of insurrection among the Jews throughout
the world," (3) "a ringleader of the sect of the
Nazarenes," (4) and, in particular, a man "who
moreover assayed to profane the temple." This bill
of particulars seemed specious enough and Tertul-

lus complimented Felix in the charge, affirming that these things were so." The case seemed made out by the accusers.

So Felix beckoned to Paul to speak in his own defense (Acts 24:10–21). He had to win a hearing by courtesy without fawning flattery. He confines himself to saying that Felix has been for many years a judge unto this nation and so he ought to be able to judge his case properly. Paul therefore makes his defense cheerfully. It is only twelve days since he went up to Jerusalem and so the events preceding his arrest are all recent. He pointedly denies all the charges save one: "Neither in the temple did they find one disputing with any man or stirring up a crowd, nor in the synagogues nor in a city." As a matter of fact, when the uproar came he was engaged in observing the rites of the temple worship. "Neither can they prove to thee the things whereof they now accuse me." They had furnished no proof and Paul was well within his rights in demanding it. Mere denunciation did not constitute proof.

But Paul had one confession to make. He did belong to "the sect of the Nazarenes." If that was a crime, then he was guilty. But Gallio, proconsul of Achaia, had decided that Christianity was a form of Judaism and so a *religio licita*. We do not know whether Paul reminded Felix of this decision or not, but Felix most likely was familiar with it. "But this I confess unto thee, that after the Way which they call a sect, so serve I the God of our fathers." Paul definitely agrees with the opinion

of Gallio and affirms to Felix that Christianity is
merely his form of Judaism. He believed the Law
and the prophets and had a hope of the resurrection
of the just and the unjust. He had kept a good conscience in his conduct toward God and men. It was
a most skillful defense. If he had stopped at this
point, Felix would have had difficulty in holding
him a prisoner. But Paul proceeded to tell the purpose of his recent visit to Jerusalem, "to bring alms
to my nation, and offerings." It is pretty clear that
this allusion to money aroused the cupidity of Felix
who saw a chance of a larger bribe to be offered by
Paul or his friends for his freedom. Paul proceeded
to give the occasion of his arrest, due to "certain
Jews from Asia, who ought to have been here before
thee, and to make accusation, if they had aught
against thee." Here Paul made a home-thrust.
These Jews from Asia made the false charge that
Paul was defiling the temple at the very moment
when he was honoring it and observing its forms
of worship. These Asiatic Jews roused the mob to
fury and then vanished, never to be heard of more.
But it will take Paul over five years to get out of
this tangled skein of false charges. But Paul turns
to the Sanhedrin, his present accusers, who are
making charges against him now before Felix. "Or
else let these men themselves say what wrong-doing
they found when I stood before the council, except
it be for this one voice, that I cried standing among
them, Touching the resurrection of the dead I am
called in question before you this day." There was
no denying that Paul had told the facts as they oc-

curred, including the onset of the Pharisees and the Sadducees on each other because Paul affirmed that he was a Pharisee still on the point of the resurrection.

The case was now before Felix and he should have set Paul free on the evidence before him. But Luke adds a remark quite in keeping with what we know of Felix: "But Felix, having more exact knowledge concerning the Way, deferred them." The meaning is probably that he knew of Gallio's decision concerning the equality of Christianity and approved it. Hence he could not condemn Paul as the Sanhedrin desired. Why did he not set him free? He feared the Jews and so left Paul a prisoner after two years, "desiring to gain favor with the Jews." He was the Roman ruler of these Jewish leaders who could make damaging charges against him as they did when he was recalled at the end of the two years when Festus succeeded him. Felix gave his judicial decision a political twist with an eye on his own interest.

But this is not all. He said, to be sure, that he would determine Paul's case after Lysias came down and he could talk the matter over with him. That sounded specious, but it was mere camouflage. What he really hoped for was money. Bribery was the quickest and the usual way to get a favorable decision from this Roman provincial judge. It is probable that Drusilla, a Jewess, and the mistress of Felix, was responsible for the coming of Paul before them for a sermon, not for trial.

She may have had some curiosity to hear him "concerning the faith of Christ Jesus" (Acts 24:24). But the effect was wholly unexpected to both Felix and Drusilla. "And as he reasoned of righteousness, and self-control, and the judgment to come, Felix was terrified." Felix is now on trial before his conscience as he listened to Paul who threw a powerful light upon his own life of evil. The time had come for Felix to settle his own account with God, but he put it off, this procrastinator, with the polite excuse: "Go thy way for this time; and when I have a convenient season, I will call thee unto me." Felix was deeply moved, but he was a grafter at heart and this master passion won the day. "He hoped withal that money would be given him of Paul: wherefore also he sent for him the oftener, and communed with him." He was never terrified again. He stifled his conscience with the hope of money. He kept sending for Paul and let him talk with the hope that Paul would offer money for his liberty. He knew, as Lysias did, that Paul was guilty of no crime. But he would not set him free. He was afraid of the Jews and he wanted money. These two reasons overcame his evident fondness for Paul and suppressed his terrified conscience and postponed indefinitely his personal interest in the faith in Christ Jesus. One could wish that Felix stood alone among the Roman governors who listened to their fears more than to their sense of justice. But the figure of Pilate rises before us. And Festus is not a whit better. Judges ought to be above partisanship, personal interest, and graft. If that were true always, conviction for crime would come with more speed and with more frequency.

CHAPTER XV

SIMON THE CRITIC OF CHRIST

(Luke 7:36–50)

THERE are few passages in Luke's wonderful Gospel more thoroughly characteristic of the author's style and spirit. Stanton (*Gospels as Historical Documents,* vii. p. 229) feels sure that here Luke is not quoting a literary document, but is telling the story in his own words. As is often the case, Luke gives no date and no place for the incident, though it does serve as a striking illustration of the sneers of the Pharisees about Christ as a glutton and a wine-bibber, a friend of publicans and sinners (Luke 7:34) and the conclusion holds true that wisdom is justified of her children (7:35).

The name Simon is very common. There are about twenty in Josephus and ten (or eleven) in the New Testament. There is no reason whatever for identifying this Pharisee with the Simon who was a leper and who gave a feast to Jesus (Mark 14:3–9; Matthew 26:6–13; John 12:2–8). It may be said also that there is no ground for confounding this sinful woman with Mary Magdalene of Luke 8:1–3 and least of all with Mary of Bethany who is so clearly pictured by Luke himself (10:39–

42). Ragg (*The Gospel according to St. Luke* p. 97) feels rather helpless over the curious confusion of artists on this subject: "In any case we may be sure that for *history* this unnamed sinner, and Mary Magdalene, and Mary of Bethany are three separate persons; though for *Art* they will probably remain one." That is only true in the sense that the ancient paintings cannot be now altered, but they undoubtedly slander both Mary Magdalene and Mary of Bethany.

But we are concerned here with the picture of Simon the Critic of Christ. Criticism of Jesus was inevitable then as it is now. Our age is one of untrammeled criticism and sifting of all data and ideas about Christ. One cannot wish it otherwise. Certainly no one wishes any fact about Jesus to be concealed or overlooked or forgotten. He could not be hid when upon earth and desiring seclusion. One does not wish Christ to be hid now. Jesus condemned captious criticism in severe terms. One does not become a scholar by reason of his gift at criticizing or picking flaws. One is not necessarily right because he is able to make sharp and specious criticism. After the messengers had started back to John the Baptist in prison Jesus gave a scathing indictment of the Pharisaic critics of the time who could not be pleased about either John or Jesus (Luke 7:24–35). They found fault with John because of his dress and his food and his unlikeness to people of the time. They found fault with Jesus because he was too much like the people of the age. The Pharisees assumed the critical attitude toward Jesus as they had the right to do. Only they had their eyes blinded by prejudice so that they could not see the light. They were unable to tell the truth when they saw it. These men who posed as the exponents of truth shut the door of truth, flung away the key, and would not let those enter into the house of knowledge who wanted to do so. They became the past-masters of obscurantism and the synonym for hypocrisy in all ages.

This Simon who invited Jesus to his house for dinner was a Pharisee and illustrates the wrong kind of criticism of Christ in a really wonderful way. He was evidently kindly disposed towards Jesus. There is nothing to indicate that he had any sinister motive in inviting Jesus to dine with him. It may (Plummer) have been a really courageous act on his part to give Jesus this invitation since the Pharisees were generally hostile. Luke mentions two other later instances where Pharisees invited Jesus to meals (Luke 11:27–54; 14:1–35). In each of the three instances the thing turned out badly. In Luke 11 the Pharisee criticized Christ for not bathing (probably dipping the hands and feet in water on entrance) before the breakfast, a criticism that led to three woes to the Pharisees and three to the lawyers. In Luke 14 the Pharisees themselves had come with hostile intentions and were on the lookout for flaws. Ragg terms "Luke's the Gospel of Hospitality." That is true, but the Pharisaic atmosphere was not very congenial to Christ. Probably this Pharisaic host had an element of self-importance in inviting Jesus as a sort of social lion and he may even have desired to know Jesus better in order to make up his mind about him (Easton).

It is clear, of course, that the woman of the town had not been invited by this particular and punctilious Pharisee. She was a well-known character who had evidently accepted Christ as her Savior (note verse 50, "Thy faith has saved thee") and wished to show her gratitude to him for her rescue from sin. She knew that public opinion still regarded her as a harlot in spite of the change of heart and life. In the orient even now uninvited guests can enter the banquet hall and stand around, but it called for courage for this woman to enter the Pharisee's house. The guests reclined at table, having dropped their sandals as they entered. This woman came in on purpose because she had learned that Jesus was to dine that day at this Pharisee's house (verse 37). So she was an intruder as Mary of Bethany was not when she anointed Jesus. This woman had the box of ointment and slipped furtively behind, but she was evidently overcome with emotion and burst into tears that fell on the feet of Jesus as she stood weeping. Then she felt that she must wipe the tears away and unloosed her long hair for that purpose. The Jews looked on loosened hair in public as a shameful thing, but she made this sacrifice (Plummer), knowing what people would think. And then she kissed His feet repeatedly and kept pouring out (imperfect tense) the ointment till it was gone. She had not acted as she had planned and the emotional excitement led to the tears, the wiping with her hair, the kissing the feet.

Meanwhile Simon, the sedate Pharisee, had watched the performance with growing amazement that his distinguished guest should allow such a scene in his house without a word of protest and of displeasure at the woman's unseemly conduct. His indignation grew apace and finally he began to draw conclusions of a thoroughgoing nature concerning the claims of Jesus to be the Messiah. Perhaps the Pharisees were right after all in their wholesale rejection of this Galilean who violated the conventions. Perhaps he had more affinity with publicans and sinners than people generally supposed. Even to-day there are not wanting critics who identify this woman with Mary Magdalene and assert that she was the mistress of Jesus, horrible insinuations we rightly feel. But there is a whole group of critics to-day who argue that Jesus was a paranoiac with definite psychic abnormalities. So hostile criticism of Jesus has always existed and always will. Jesus challenged the fullest investigation. He asked the disciples what men thought of him and then what *they* themselves thought of him. In itself criticism simply means sifting and that process is necessary in making all right decisions.

What was the trouble with this Pharisee when "he said in himself" what he did about Jesus? He drew the conclusion about the character and claims of Christ from a false interpretation of this one incident. He said in his heart: "This fellow, if he were a prophet, would know who and what sort the woman is who is clinging to him, because she is a sinner." There is a sneer in the contemptuous use of the pronoun. The condition belongs to the second class which states the thing as untrue (determined as unfulfilled). A Greek conditional sentence puts the thing according to the conception of the user, not according to the actual facts. In this instance Jesus is the prophet and does know the character of the woman. But Simon puts it as he sees it. The conclusion drawn so positively by Simon is that Jesus is ignorant of the character of the woman and therefore is not a prophet (least of all, *the* prophet, as some manuscripts have it). If he were the Messiah, he would know better. Even if he were a prophet, he would not be so ignorant. He was shocked (Ragg) along with the others to see Jesus "submitting to these defiling caresses." There is no finer illustration anywhere of the folly of posing as omniscient under the influence of prejudice that flies off the handle at small provocation. Simon ridicules Jesus in his heart because he allows no other motive for the conduct of Jesus than ignorance. Simon is incapable of comprehending the love, pity, and forgiveness of Christ as the explanation of his conduct. Simon is not the first or the last critic of Christ who has such a narrow grasp of the facts that he draws a wholly erroneous conclusion. It is one of the monumental follies of scholarship that a specialist is necessarily correct. We need specialists in every line of learning and of business. But no class of men show more nar-

rowness than some specialists who are unable to
see anything beyond the one item under observa-
tion. Diagnosis is the first step in therapeutics.
Doctors do not always agree in that and they dis-
agree often in the treatment of the disease. But
dogmatism about disease is no worse than dogmatism in theology when one is in possession of only
one fact. The only safety lies in criticizing the
critic of Christ.

This Jesus proceeds to do. Jesus not only knows
the character of this woman, her present repentance as well as her past sin, but he reads the
thoughts of Simon like a book. With Socratic irony
(Godet) Jesus lays bare Simon's inmost doubts
with the surgeon's scalpel. Probably his very face
revealed to Jesus the thoughts of his heart, but
Jesus knew what was in man without a spoken
word. Calling his critic and host by name Jesus
says: "Simon, I have something to say to thee."
Simon was probably still a bit contemptuous and
shocked. Easton thinks that what Jesus did may
be misunderstood as "a gentle correction of a natural error." It is to me far from gentle, but Simon
could only say: "Teacher, speak," with all outward
politeness and courtesy.

The reply of Jesus takes the form of a parable, a
pungent and powerful one, The Parable of the Two
Debtors. In this instance Jesus not only told the
inimitable little story, but he made direct application in the most unmistakable manner. It was a
moment of tension. The unfortunate woman was
standing at the feet of Jesus. The attention of

the guests was alert. Simon himself was on the *qui vive*. The story (verses 41 and 42) is crisp and cutting. The creditor *forgave* both the debtors. That was the point that Simon had overlooked in his wrong inference. Simon is put on the defensive by the pointed question of Jesus in a way that he cannot evade as to which of the debtors will love more. His reply is inevitable even if his air is that of supercilious indifference (Plummer). Ragg thinks that he was merely polite, but not really interested when he said: "I suppose." But at any rate he saw the point and admitted it, which is not always true of those who listen to stories. The moral of the story was self-evident and the Pharisee admitted it and Jesus commended him for doing so: "You have judged rightly." But Jesus did not stop with the mere answer to a conundrum. He turned to the woman and spoke to Simon in a way to make the contrast as sharp as possible. Jesus pointed out three items wherein Simon had failed in common courtesy to Jesus as his invited guest. He had provided no water for His feet, no kiss of greeting, no oil for the head. The woman had wet His feet with her tears and wiped them with her hair, she had kissed His feet, and she had anointed His feet with ointment. The sarcasm of Jesus was positively biting. But Jesus not only exposed the narrow criticism of Simon in the presence of all the guests, but he also further justified His conduct towards the woman in allowing her to show her grateful love in her own exceptional way. This statement of Jesus has been much misunderstood. Roman Catholic commentators take verse 47 to mean that her many sins have been forgiven because of her much love, the doctrine of *contritio caritate formata,* and the pictures of the Magdalene grew out of it. The language of verse 47 is capable of that meaning if it stood by itself, but verse 48 flatly contradicts it: "He to whom little is forgiven loves little." This is the point of the parable and of Christ's justification of the conduct of the woman and of his treatment of her. Her much love is proof of the great forgiveness, not the ground or reason of the forgiveness. Her sins were many and have been forgiven. Hence her love is great. This is the clear meaning of Jesus in his wonderful interpretation of the Parable of the Two Debtors as a final reply to Simon the Critic. Simon was left overwhelmed as all shallow critics of Christ will be some day when they stand in the full glare of all the facts.

But Jesus has a further word to the penitent woman: "Thy sins stand forgiven" (perfect passive indicative, a state of completion). The critical sneer of Simon cannot change this essential fact. Thank God for that. In the welter of carping criticism of Christ all about us he stands calm and victorious. The guests at the banquet are now heard from. They had seen and heard all that had transpired, but now they had troubles of their own. Jesus now actually assumed the right to forgive sins, a divine prerogative as they understood it. And yet they dared not speak out aloud what they were thinking within themselves: "Who is this who even forgives sins?" But Jesus had in reality answered their thoughts by what he had said. He does not stop to answer their puzzled minds. We sometimes wonder why God leaves us with so much perplexity. He means us to use our minds if we can and get the good out of perplexity. Life is a matter largely of balancing probabilities and making the right choice. So Jesus has a final word for the woman: "Go in peace." We are not told what happened to the meal after this. That is a small matter, important as such a function seems at the moment.

CHAPTER XVI

MARTHA AND MARY OR TEMPERAMENT IN RELIGION

THE Bethany family included Martha, Mary and Lazarus. The names are common enough, but these were very unusual persons. They were all unmarried and lived together in a home of evident comfort if not affluence. The great number of prominent Jews who came out to comfort the sisters upon the death of Lazarus (John 11:19, 31) shows that the family was one of prominence in social life. The great cost of Mary's offering proves that she had considerable ready money. Martha apparently was the head of the household if we may judge from Luke 10:38 where Martha possibly a widow (Easton), acts as hostess. The glory of this family is that they provided a home for Jesus during his later Jerusalem ministry. He had withdrawn from Galilee because of the hostility of the populace. It was a time when Jesus said that the foxes had holes and the birds had nests, but the son of Man had not where to lay his head. But there was always one place near Jerusalem, the very seat of the ecclesiastic opposition to Jesus, where he found a welcome. There are always some people who have the courage to take a stand in the open for Jesus and for all that he means for men. There came loss of prestige to this family after the raising of Lazarus for the rulers conspired to put him to death as well as Jesus because of the interest in Jesus created by this miracle.

But the two sisters are the chief figures in the family and their pictures are drawn by Luke and by John. They have all the marks of reality, a striking "undesigned coincidence" (Ragg), because, though John and Luke differ in method and style, yet each draws these sisters with characteristic individuality. Evidently characters so true to the life in each book were drawn from actual personages. They appear in three remarkable scenes, once as hostesses in the home (Luke 10:38-42), once when great grief broke their hearts (John 11:17-44), once as guests in the home of a friend (Mark 14:3-9, Matthew 26:6-13, John 12:2-8).

Each acts in perfect accord with herself in each instance and each is sharply distingushed from the other. The keen differences of conduct are largely due to variations in temperament which are deep and permanent. Lightfoot (*Biblical Essays,* pg. 38) has a fine word concerning the way Luke and John have noted the distinction between Mary and Martha: "But these characteristics of the two sisters are brought out in a very subtle way. In St. Luke the contrast is summed up, as it were in one definite incident; in St. John it is developed gradually in the course of a continuous narrative. In St. Luke the contrast is direct and trenchant, a contrast (one might almost say) of light and darkness. But in St. John the characters are shaded off, as it were, into one another." It is not necessary to find types of creed or of doctrine in these two noble women. They do admirably illustrate the different reactions found in women and men to all religious truth. They both felt the charm and the appeal of Christ, but they responded in different ways. There is personality in religion as in all else. Many of the tragedies and sorrows of the ages have been due to unwise and impossible efforts to regulate each other often in more or less unimportant matters. People have different eyes and do not see alike when they look at the same object. People have different minds and cannot think alike about the same things. This does not mean that one view is as good as another. Jesus Christ is the same yesterday, to-day and forever. But each one has his own angle of vision and is entitled to the experience that he has.

Mary and Martha did not always understand one another's attitude toward Jesus. There is a phrase often used about unhappy marriages, incompatibility of temperament, that does not justify divorce, but throws some light on family jars. Some people seem not to know how to live together without explosions, whether in family, church, school or state. Sometimes it is a matter of nerves that improves with better health. Overstrain explains much of the unpleasantness of life. A vacation has the great merit of change of environment and outlook and thereafter the common tasks seem less onerous. Much of life is a study in adaptation to one's environment. Worry wears out the nerves more than work and makes work difficult.

In the first incident (Luke 10:38–42) Martha acted as hostess and welcomed Jesus to her house as the margin has it in Westcott and Hort's text and as the article really means even without the pronoun. That is her rôle throughout, while Mary appears rather as the adoring disciple who sat (right down beside and facing) at the feet of Jesus and listened in rapture (imperfect tense) to his wondrous talk. But Luke has one little word ("also") that is commonly overlooked. Weiss and Easton take it to refer to Mary's eagerness while Plummer is uncertain what the precise idea is, though certainly not "even." The most natural way of taking it is that Martha as well as Mary loved to sit at the feet of Jesus, but gradually the household duties engrossed her more while Mary followed her bent and devoted herself more to the delights of listening to Jesus talk. Each followed her own inclination and each justified herself in doing mainly the one thing because of the conduct of the other. Mary's continual sitting at the feet of Jesus led to Martha's monotonous devotion to the drudgery of household duties till it became a habit with her that began to show on her face and on her nerves. She was literally "drawn around" (imperfect tense as the verb picturesquely says, "distracted") because of the much serving. The inevitable explosion came suddenly, as is usually the case. Martha stopped her work, stepped up to

Jesus and burst out with what seemed like a rebuke to him for having allowed Mary to act as she
had been doing. Martha said: "Do you not care
that my sister had been leaving me alone to go on
serving?" Her temper and petulance were plain.
She went on: "Bid her therefore that she take hold
(ingressive aorist subjunctive) along with me" (a
double compound verb that occurs also in Romans
8:26 about the help of the Holy Spirit, and one
common in the vernacular *Koine* of the time).
Martha was plainly tired of doing all the work
while Mary did nothing but listen and talk. It was
a most embarrassing moment in the life of this de-
lightful family where Jesus was most welcome and
felt most at home. At such a moment most of us
are wise in preferring silence. But Jesus had been
directly appealed to and even directly blamed so
that there was no way of escape. So the Lord replied to Martha's outburst briefly, but pungently:
"Martha, Martha, you are anxious and bustling
about many things." The repetition of the name
was a gentle chiding, perhaps with a smile (Ragg).
The Syriac Sinaitic manuscript omits the chiding
entirely, but it is probably genuine. Her anxiety
was natural, but was overdone and had led to the
explosive disturbance that she had just made. The
external agitation was due to the mental distrac-
tion (Plummer). Jesus goes on, but the text is uncertain: "There is need of few things (instead of
the many dishes planned by Martha, kindly but
mistaken hospitality seen often in elaborate
'spreads' at table) or one" (with a double meaning,

as Plummer shows, even one is enough for a meal, and this one is illustrated in a spiritual way by what Mary has done). It is possible that the oldest text was "one" or "few" which were both combined into "few or one." But the one thing needful directly refers to the one dish on which a meal can be made in place of the great variety contemplated by Martha. But the next clause gives the full justification of Mary by Jesus and carries the figure of the one dish into the spiritual realm: "For Mary chose the good portion which will not be taken away from her." Jesus here definitely declines to do what Martha asked. He will not forbid Mary's sitting at his feet in order that he may have more to eat. Martha's distracting anxiety was the result of affection (Plummer), but all the same between the two extremes Jesus preferred the conduct of Mary to that of Martha. Jesus did not condemn the service that Martha had rendered, but only her finding fault with Mary and her undue excited state of mind. She had definitely stepped beyond her prerogative in trying to make Mary conform to her own habits of life. It is a curiosity of modern criticism when the Tübingen school deny the historical character of the narrative and take Martha to represent Judaic Christianity and Mary Pauline Christianity or Martha the impulsive Peter and Mary the philosophic Paul (see Plummer). Dante caught the conception of the two sisters more nearly when he said: "Do as you are doing, but do not fret about it: Mary also is doing the right thing." Martha is thus a type of the active, Mary of the contemplative life. Christ here preaches the simple life.

In John 11 the two sisters again are true to life. Luke had not named the village as John does, but John calls Bethany the village of Mary and Martha as if they were the chief characters of the town. The sickness and death of Lazarus cast a shadow over this home and Jesus was away apparently a journey of two days (John 11:6, 17) in Perea. It seemed almost heartless to the agonized sisters that Jesus did not come at once when he received the message that Lazarus was at the point of death. They did not know what Jesus told the disciples that he remained away on purpose (John 11:6) and let Lazarus die "that the son of God might be glorified" thereby (John 11:4). One is permitted to cherish the hope that in the midst of like sorrows the Son of God may be glorified in ways that we do not understand. The two sisters did not doubt the love of Jesus for Lazarus and for themselves nor his power to prevent the death of their brother. Evidently they had talked the problem over with each other because each of them said separately to Jesus: "Lord, if thou hadst been here, my brother would not have died" (John 11:21, 32). It was to them unthinkable that Jesus would let Lazarus die if He were present. But, now that he had been dead these four days, it was not so certain what He would do. We do not know what the sisters knew concerning the raising of the daughter of Jairus and the son of the widow of Nain. The practical Martha went right out to see Jesus as soon as she

learned that he had come (11:20). She even sug-
gested to Jesus the raising of Lazarus from the
dead by an exhibition of the most marvelous faith:
"And even now I know that whatsoever thou shalt
ask of God, God will give it thee." What was Jesus
to do with this challenge of Martha to his love
and his power? It was not a time for mere argument or dialectical fencing and yet it was necessary
to prove Martha's faith and mental attitude. So
Jesus said to her: "Thy brother will rise again."
But this promise of the general resurrection hope
did not satisfy Martha's present needs. So she replied: "I know that he will arise at the resurrection
on the last day." Jesus now explained his meaning
with a marvelous claim to Martha, the power to
give eternal life to him: "I am the resurrection and
the life," words that astound us to-day with their
amazing implications. Jesus had a way of saying
the most profound things in an incidental way to
individuals as to Nicodemus and to the Samaritan
woman at the well. These words fully justified Martha's hope, but Jesus proceeded with a double sense
of life and death: "He that believeth in me even if
he die (physical death) shall live (spiritual life),
and no one who believes in me shall ever die (spiritual life)." It was still not clear what Jesus meant
to do for Martha. But he suddenly put her faith to
the severest possible test: "Believest thou this?" or
"Is this your belief?" What had Jesus meant to
claim to Martha? The power to give eternal life to
every one who believes on him beyond a doubt. Had
he also claimed the power to raise Lazarus from

the dead here and now? Not in so many words, but
he had implied it by saying: "I am the resurrection
and the life." And Jesus could not mean to mock
the hope of Martha. She falls back upon the confession of her faith in which she has rested for long,
the best that any of us can do in a great crisis:
"Yea, Lord, I have believed (state of completion,
perfect tense) that thou art the Messiah, the Son
of God, who was to come into the world" (John
11:27). This settled conviction explains why she
had said what she did (11:22). Simon had made a
great confession on Mount Hermon (Matt. 16ff.),
but no one ever made such a confesssion under more
trying conditions than did Martha. If Jesus meant
to raise Lazarus, he was evidently putting Martha
to a severe test beforehand and she fully realized
it. But she rose to the occasion in a magnificent
fashion. We need to add this strong side of her
faith and character to the nervous petulance ex-
hibited in Luke 10:38–42. This is permanent with
her, that was temporary. We must not allow the
natural revulsion of Martha by the tomb of Lazarus (John 11:39f.) to obscure her really great
faith. That was an instinctive recoil under the obvious environment. Jesus gently rebuked that mo-
mentary doubt with the reminder of his promise
to her that she should see the glory of God. Martha,
like most of us, had her moods of confidence and of
depression, but she rose to great heights of faith
in the presence of death. The picture of Mary is
drawn with equal vividness, and shows her characteristic traits. Martha told her that the Teacher

had come and was calling for her. So she quickly arose and went on out to see Jesus. All that Mary could say as she fell at the feet of Jesus was the lament already made by Martha (John 11:32). She was weeping without further words. What can Jesus say to Mary? He could argue with Martha's robust faith, but he could not with Mary. He treats each according to her temperament. The hostile Jews were there also and their presence called for self-control if he was to comfort Mary. But the very effort at self-mastery in such an atmosphere made Jesus burst into tears (ingressive aorist). After all what else can one do with a weeping woman but weep with her? We do not have to say that Mary was hysterical and should not have given way to her grief or that her grief was greater than that of Martha or that Jesus loved Mary more than he did Martha. Sympathy is fellow-suffering, entering into one's mood and taking a stand with one. Martha's practical nature sought a solution for her sorrow and Jesus met her on that plane. Mary's heart was all broken and bleeding. Her hurt was too deep for words, even words from Jesus. Jesus gave her His tears, real tears of human love and sympathy. But then He went on to the grave of Lazarus and raised him from the dead. That was the answer to Martha's query and the confirmation of her faith. That act stopped the flow of Mary's tears. That act led many of the Jews to believe on Jesus and led also to His own crucifixion (John 11:45–53).

The last time that we see Martha and Mary is

at the feast of Simon the former leper in gratitude
to Jesus (Mark 14:3-9, Matthew 26:6-13, John
12:2-8). This was at Bethany near Jerusalem on
Tuesday evening of Passion Week according to the
Synoptic Gospels. It was a remarkable company
including Jesus and the twelve apostles and the
Bethany sisters and Lazarus. It has been held by
some that Martha was the wife of Simon because
she "served" on the occasion. But that is unneces-
sary and wholly unlikely in view of Martha's own
separate home in Bethany. She here is merely true
to her own practical nature as already seen on the
other occasions. It is Mary who plays the important
rôle at this feast. Her act was premeditated and
prearranged. The whole room was filled with the
odor of the ointment poured on the head and the
feet of Jesus. It was Judas Iscariot (John 12:4)
who made violent protest against this "waste" of
money that might have been used for the poor, a
protest supported by the other disciples after it
was made (Matt. 26:8) as "they murmured against
her" (Matt. 14:5). It was a most embarrassing
moment for Mary. She had poured out her very
heart's love in this act of devotion with thoughts
full of the death of the Master of which he had
spoken so often and of which the apostles seemed to
have no proper appreciation. And now she has had
this public rebuke from the preachers who should
have understood her. What if Jesus shared the
same feeling? But she had not long to wait. Jesus
sharply rebuked Judas and the rest and defended
Mary for showing her love in her own way. "She

hath done what she could." These words have gone with the story of the gospel through the ages as Christ's memorial for Mary's deed of love (Mark 14:9). She had anointed Christ beforehand for his burial while the disciples had utterly failed to understand his words about his death. Here Mary rises to the heights with her temperament of mystical insight as Martha stood firm in the hour of despair and of the death of Lazarus. Later the disciples came to understand their own shortsightedness and to see that Judas was all wrong because a thief in fact (John 12:6) and had misled them by his concealed stinginess in opposition to Mary's generosity and nobility of sentiment.

The supreme lesson for modern men and women in the lives of Martha and Mary is precisely that of toleration, forbearance, liberty in matters of personal idiosyncrasy and outlook. The two sisters loved Jesus with equal sincerity and devotion, but they showed their love in very different ways. It is not going too far to say that denominations have arisen on less important differences than existed between Martha and Mary. Compulsory uniformity on all points is impossible in the family, in the church, in the state. It is a distinctly modern problem to learn when to be firm, when to be tolerant. Law is necessary in essential things if we are to have stability in society, but love must carry on for the rest. They say that no two leaves are precisely alike and yet it is not difficult to tell a maple leaf from that of the oak or the elm. Temperament in religion gives the variety of life and the joy of independence. We must never forget that Jesus loved Martha and that he loved Mary, that he treated each according to her temperament, and that he did not attempt to make either of them like the other.

CHAPTER XVII

ANANIAS AND SAPPHIRA OR THE FIRST ANANIAS CLUB

(Acts 5:1–11)

FEW things in the Acts have caught the popular imagination like the story of Ananias and Sapphira. The couple had lovely names Ananias (to whom Jehovah has been gracious), Sapphira (either a sapphire or the Aramaic word for beautiful). But names play a very small part in one's actual life. It was another Ananias in Damascus who was charged with the duty of opening the eyes of Saul who was stopping at the home of one Judas. Undoubtedly Ananias and Sapphira before the incident in Acts 5 bore a good reputation in the Jerusalem church.

It is a bit remarkable (Rackham) how large a part the greed for gain played in the book of Acts. The sin of Achan and of Gehazi reappears here in the life of Ananias and Sapphira as we see it also in Simon Magus, Elynas, the masters of the poor girl in Philippi, Demetrius of Ephesus, the chicanery of Felix. Certainly the love of money is a root of all kinds of evil.

Luke does not hesitate to tell the unvarnished

168

facts about this sin in the early church in Jerusalem. He lets the facts speak for themselves and makes no effort to gloss it over with any pious platitudes or excuses. The incident stands out in sharp contrast to the noble deed of Joseph Barnabas whose generosity undoubtedly was the occasion for the evil act of Ananias and Sapphira. It is plain that the disciples of this early period were not immune to the darts of the devil. Rackham wrongly uses Luke's fidelity in recording the facts about Ananias and Sapphira as a protest against the effort "to found new and 'pure' churches," though he admits that "against this experience of the kingdom of God spiritually minded men have risen in all ages." It is true that in the Acts we see in the life of the disciples themselves first hypocrisy (V), then murmuring (VI), then dissension and contention (XV). But the leaders like Peter and Paul did not commend the practice of evil in the churches. Certainly it is small consolation to know that the tares do grow among the wheat, for the field is the world as Jesus taught. The final separation comes only at death and the judgment. The good and the evil live together in the world. This is no argument against church discipline or cleansing, but it is one against pessimism. We often speak of the good old times, but forget that evils existed then as well as now. No halo of glory can cover up the selfish greed and ambitious pride observable in the tragic careers of Ananias and Sapphira over money and church money at that.

It is clear that the hearty praise given by the

church to Joseph Barnabas excited Ananias and Sapphira to follow his example. Barnabas was a man of considerable wealth and he voluntarily sold his piece of property and laid the money at the feet of the apostles (Acts 4:37). It is small wonder that he was called the Son of Consolation for this timely liberality. The communism practised by the Christians at Jerusalem was voluntary and was used only as need required. It was in no sense compulsory and does not seem to have been practised elsewhere. But human nature changes little in its essential features through the ages.

Ananias and Sapphira felt that their social standing entitled them to as much praise as Barnabas had received. They talked the matter over and decided to sell their property and keep back part of it and to give the other part as if it was the whole price of the property sold. It was duplicity, but they thought it would not be known. Then they proceeded to put the plan into execution like the little boy who wanted to keep his cake and eat it too. They wanted all the credit and applause that had been bestowed upon Barnabas without the deprivation of absolutely all this property. So Ananias brought the money (part of it) and laid it ostentatiously at the feet of the apostles as Barnabas had done and waited for the commendation that Barnabas had received. It was thus a deliberate offense, his wife knowing all that he was doing. Satan had entered his heart and had obscured the real nature of his sin. It was not merely purloining, bad as that is. It was lying, acting a lie.

He was not doing the truth (I John 1:6). He was doing a lie (Rev. 22:15). He was trying to serve God and mammon like Deacon Skinflint who asked the grocer boy to come on to prayers if he had put sand in the sugar and rocks in the coffee. Here was the same type of hypocrisy in some in the Jerusalem church that Jesus had so strongly condemned in the Pharisees, the pious pretense that was more concerned with the outward show than the inward reality.

It was a shock to Ananias when Simon Peter suddenly exposed his hollow pretense to the whole church. The Holy Spirit was unwilling for this pious fraud to go through and revealed it to Peter, who spoke out with courage and power. Ananias had lied to the Holy Spirit in keeping back part of the price of the property. Peter argued the matter with him, though it was too late. He did not have to sell it nor did he have to give it after it was sold. This point proves that it was not compulsory or legal communism. It was certainly proper for Ananias to give half of his property which is far more than most modern Christians do. The sin lay, not in giving part, but in giving part as if it were all and expecting credit for giving all. Peter is amazed that Ananias could have conceived such a base falsehood, a lie not merely to men (bad as that is) but a lie to God. Satan had put it into the heart of Ananias, but that suggestion of the Devil in no sense absolved Ananias of his responsibility for the sin.

One can easily imagine how Ananias quailed before this terrible exposure of the secret ambition of his heart. It is not said that Peter smote him with death. Paul called down blindness on Elymas Barjesus as Peter condemned Simon Magus. But without any sentence from Peter, Ananias suddenly fell down and gave up the ghost. He fell as he was listening to the words of Peter. The physical cause of his death is not clear. On physiological grounds it is not hard to conceive that the sudden revulsion of emotion burst a blood vessel and caused apoplexy as he was listening to Peter's denunciation. But, natural as all this may be, the sudden death was the judgment of God for the wickedness of Ananias.

The effect upon the people was great and instantaneous. The people were full of fear and it affected the whole church (first use of the word church in the critical text of Acts) and all the people paused and pondered before they rushed heedlessly into the membership of a body like this where one was expected to walk so straight a line.

The burial of Ananias within three hours seems undue haste to us, but in Jerusalem the interval between death and burial was brief (Numbers 19: 11, Deut. 21:23). Furneaux considers it inconceivable that a man of substance like Ananias could be put into the tomb so quickly and without the knowledge of his wife. But sometimes the body was placed in a temporary tomb or vault before final burial. We know too little about ancient customs to call it cruel and heartless or incredible.

The younger men stand out in contrast to the elders, very much like active pall bearers to-day or the ushers in some churches. It is not certain that already there was a definite body of church workers called the younger men by way of anticipation of the deacons. Then young men did the honors of the burial. They placed the limbs together, wrapped the body round with some robe and decently bore it out and buried it.

But the incident was not over. Without knowing how matters had gone with Ananias, Sapphira, (his wife,) came in after an interval of some three hours. She may (Noesgen) have come in at the next hour of prayer. But at once she subjected to a direct query by Peter: "Did you sell the land for so much?" He probably named the price as that of the money laid at his feet by Ananias. She was thus given the opportunity to tell the truth about it and to retract the lying agreement with her husband about it. She had her chance to come clean without knowing the fate of Ananias. But she persisted in the sin and spoke plainly the lie that Ananias had acted by deed. She stuck to the nefarious compact and Peter instantly foretold her fate. But he first expressed his amazement at the depth of depravity that led her and her husband to agree together to tempt the Spirit of the Lord. Probably they had not realized that they were really doing this thing. Usually sin blurs the mental and spiritual perceptions so that the worse appears the better reason. To them the end justified the means in this case. They felt that they were entitled to as much prestige as Joseph Barnabas had achieved.

Certainly the solemn prediction that "the feet of those who buried thy husband are at the door and they will bear thee out" was a shock equal to that received by Ananias. Her immediate death was the judgment of God upon her for her share in the common sin as was the sudden death of Ananias. The same young men, though a different word is employed, that had buried Ananias came in and found her dead and bore her out and buried her beside her husband.

It was a tragic dénouement to the sinful conduct that had promised them so much pleasure and profit. If one is disposed to question the love and justice of God for this quick retribution for secret wrongdoing, he can gain some light by reflecting upon the evil consequences in American life to-day of the slow and uncertain processes in our legal procedure when technicalities often give loopholes for the escape of the guilty and for the consequent spread of crime. This was the first social sin in the life of the Jerusalem church of which we know. The sin was primarily against God. The exposure was by the Holy Spirit to Simon Peter. The local church had no experience to guide them. This sin cut to the very vitals of the church life and made a mockery of all that was true in Christianity. When one considers all these things, the severe judgment of the Holy Spirit through Simon Peter is more intelligible to us.

The effect upon the whole church was most salu-
tary. A great and wholesome fear came upon the
whole community and they all saw that hypocrisy
could not pass muster in the kingdom of God. The
new church had its justification for existing as an
effort to carry on the ideals and standards of Jesus
Christ who had denounced so vigorously the hypocritical Pharisees. But hypocritical disciples of
Jesus were far worse for the very reason that they
made higher claims to purity of life. They had the
example of Jesus before them and the promise of
the Holy Spirit to cheer and help and hold them
to the highest.

Another result was that this incident gave pause
to all the outsiders who heard these things. It was
already becoming with some a popular thing to
become disciples of Jesus. If it meant death for
slips like that made by Ananias and Sapphira, it
was a serious and solemn thing to join such an
organization as the Jerusalem church. One had
best search his own heart carefully before he
stumbled into a thing that might have such tragic
consequences. This was all to the good and a wholesome restraint came that sifted out the superficial
timeservers who did not have the root of the matter in them. The appeal was all the stronger to
the courageous who all the more believed in the
Lord Jesus and took an open stand for him (Acts
5:14). That is always the case in times of testing
and Christ calls the high-minded souls who are
willing to take risks for him. The appeal is made
to the heroic so that in all the Christian centuries

as at the first multitudes of young men and young women of the very highest types have gladly laid their lives at the feet of Jesus for service wherever he needed them most.

It is a curious bit of history that the very name of Ananias has been used for what we call an Ananias Club, a bunch of real liars, or a group so denominated by their opponents. But he deserved this fate for his name because he did get his wife Sapphira to agree to the despicable plot for selfish promotion in the church life by lying even to the Holy Spirit.

CHAPTER XVIII

Lazarus the Silent Witness of the Secrets of Death

There was never a keener interest in the future life than there is to-day. Thomas A. Edison has actually been carrying on a scientific investigation to see if he can find evidence of a survival after death. Because he has not been able to find material proof of such survival he doubts its reality, a very unscientific conclusion and one that refuses to recognize any differences between matter and spirit. The thin wall between matter and spirit should make one cautious. The very electrons and ether offer a warning.

On the other hand a scientist like Sir Oliver Lodge claims that he has had communications with his son Raymond in the other world. He holds to this view with full faith in the claims of Christ and Christianity. But Sir Conan Doyle puts spiritualism in the place of Christianity and is a protagonist for knowledge to be derived from spiritualistic mediums concerning the future life. They both bear witness to the perennial interest in the life beyond the grave, however bizarre their ideas appear to us. It is certainly curious, to go no further, that such spiritualistic revelations can be

had only in the dark and with many proven instances of trickery and fraud.

Far back in Job's time the Lord said to him:
"Have the gates of death been revealed unto thee?
Or hast thou seen the gates of the shadow of
death?" (Job 38:17). Job did not know what was
beyond the grave. The Jewish conception of Sheol,
or the grave, was that it was darkness beyond the
gates of the shadow of death. The very image
used in Matthew 16:18 by Jesus appears in Job
38:17 and in Psalm 89:48 except that the Greek
word Hades takes the place of Sheol. The Greeks
called the unseen world Hades.

But people through all the ages have longed for
one to come back from the grave and tell what
they have seen on the other side. In the Parable
of the Rich Man and Lazarus (the other Lazarus,
not he of the Bethany family) the Rich Man who
is now in Hades and in torment begs Abraham to
send Lazarus to the house of his father and to
warn his five brothers that they may not come into
the place of torment (Luke 16:27 and 28). It was
a natural wish, but Abraham replies: "They have
Moses and the prophets; let them hear them." We
have still more. We have Jesus and the witness
of the apostles. The Rich Man continued his plead-
ing along the line of modern spiritualism: "Nay,
Father Abraham, but if one from the dead go to
them, they will repent." That sounds like a specious plea, but all history is against it. Abraham
answered: "If they do not hear Moses and the

prophets, not even will they be persuaded if one
rise from the dead."

The supreme illustration of this fact is the case
of Jesus himself. His resurrection from the dead
was a necessity to fulfill his own prediction that
he would rise from the dead on the third day after
his crucifixion. We all observe how difficult it was
for Jesus to convince his own disciples that he had
really risen from the grave, vital as that fact is
to real Christianity. And Jesus did not appear to
any of those who did not already believe in him
except in the case of Saul of Tarsus, who was already kicking against the goad. And to-day many
people profess that they would believe in Jesus
as a great prophet and teacher of ethics if they
did not have to believe in his supernatural birth
and resurrection from the grave, a spineless belief
that leaves Jesus making false claims about himself.

But the Gospel of John gives the tremendous
miracle of the Raising of Lazarus from the grave
after he had been dead four days. There is no
more difficulty in believing this miracle than the
other raisings from the dead. Jesus claimed to
have the power of life and death, to be himself the
resurrection and the life. But the admission of the
historical character of John 11 which narrates this
wondrous event carries with it the consideration
of the attitude of the people towards Lazarus, who
had been raised from the dead in such a public
manner before crowds of prominent Jews from Je-

rusalem. Many believed on Jesus because of it. Others went to the Sanhedrin and told them of their faltering faith in Judaism and their leaning toward Christ. The Sanhedrin in desperation called a meeting and said: "If we leave him (Jesus) alone thus, all men will believe on him and will take away both our place and the nation's." The raising of Lazarus had the immediate effect of making the Sanhedrin decide to put Jesus to death. So Jesus left the vicinity of Jerusalem.

But when he returned some weeks later at the fatal passover Lazarus is the object of excited interest to the visitors from afar who all hear of the tremendous event. A great multitude came out to Bethany not merely to see Jesus who is again the guest of the Bethany family, but "to see Lazarus whom he had raised from the dead" (John 12:9). Who can blame this curiosity on the part of crowds at the passover? A well authenticated case like that to-day would make a stir that would throw even Lindbergh into the shade. The Sanhedrin were enraged afresh and determined to kill both Lazarus and Jesus (John 12:10). With both of them dead, they argued, Lazarus would stay dead this second time. Because of Lazarus as a live specimen of Christ's supernatural power "many of the Jews were going and believing on Jesus" (John 12:11). Once again Lazarus has become a thorn in the side of the Sanhedrin.

The only other appearance of Lazarus in the narrative is at the feast in Bethany given by Simon, the one time leper, in honor of Jesus. He was simply one of the guests on this occasion (John 12:2). But there is not a word given in John's Gospel of anything said by Lazarus about the life beyond the grave. There was the keenest curiosity to see a man who had really come back from the grave. But not a word from the other side. The Rich Man had hoped that the messenger sent to his brothers might bear witness to them about his own sad state. But the testimony of Lazarus is only the silent witness of one who declined to be garrulous about trivial nonentities such as fill up the talk of mediums. Lazarus did not need to say anything to show that it was he who was back in human life. That was a manifest fact to all. But he had not a word to say, so far as we know, concerning what people are so anxious to know. There is dignity in this silence that puts to shame the modern efforts to prove the existence of the other life. The raising of Lazarus proved the essential fact. Here he was again as all could see.

There is one who does speak clear words concerning the future life and that is Jesus. Before his death he was conscious of his preëxistence with the Father. He has told us the really essential things concerning heaven and hell. If one will run through the Gospels to see, he may be surprised to find how much Jesus has said about the future life. He has lifted the veil for us on all really vital matters, but he has not satisfied idle curiosity in any way. It is a reflection on Christ for one to credit table-rappings and such things more than the clear and sure word of Jesus Christ who came to us from the bosom of the Father and who has gone back to the Father and who will take us to be with him in the Father's house. He did not tell the disciples all that they wished to know, but more than they at first fully comprehended and then he gave them and us the Holy Spirit to be our Guide and Teacher.

Lazarus has been credited by some scholars with the authorship of the Fourth Gospel. I do not myself believe it as the Apostle John wrote the book in my opinion. But even so, if Lazarus did write it, his silence is all the more remarkable. He left it to Jesus in any case to be the speaker to us about the life beyond the grave.

THE END